DEALING
WITH STRESS

EMPOWERING YOU

The Rowman & Littlefield *Empowering You* series is aimed to help you, as a young adult, deal with important topics that you, your friends, or family might be facing. Whether you are looking for answers about certain illnesses, social issues, or personal problems, the books in this series provide you with the most up-to-date information. Throughout each book you will also find stories from other teenagers to provide personal perspectives on the subject.

DEALING WITH STRESS

Insights and Tips for Teenagers

CHRISTIE COGNEVICH

ROWMAN & LITTLEFIELD
Lanham • Boulder • New York • London

Published by Rowman & Littlefield
An imprint of The Rowman & Littlefield Publishing Group, Inc.
4501 Forbes Boulevard, Suite 200, Lanham, Maryland 20706
www.rowman.com

86-90 Paul Street, London EC2A 4NE, United Kingdom

British Library Cataloguing in Publication Information Available

Library of Congress Cataloging-in-Publication Data

Names: Cognevich, Christie, 1984– author.
Title: Dealing with stress : insights and tips for teenagers / Christie Cognevich.
Description: Lanham : Rowman & Littlefield Publishing Group, [2022] | Series: Empowering you | Includes bibliographical references and index. | Summary: "Teens today are dealing with stress at an unprecedented level, but they are not alone. This valuable resource offers practical coping strategies, useful resources, and insight from fellow teenagers to help young adults recognize and manage stress factors in their lives"—Provided by publisher.
Identifiers: LCCN 2021057520 (print) | LCCN 2021057521 (ebook) | ISBN 9781538152850 (paperback) | ISBN 9781538152867 (epub)
Subjects: LCSH: Stress in adolescence. | Stress management for teenagers.
Classification: LCC BF724.3.S86 C624 2022 (print) | LCC BF724.3.S86 (ebook) | DDC 155.9/0420835—dc23/eng/20211217
LC record available at https://lccn.loc.gov/2021057520
LC ebook record available at https://lccn.loc.gov/2021057521

For Jen, Mary, and Willow
Thank you for the love and laughter while my spirit was wintering

CONTENTS

AUTHOR NOTE

This is a book about stress, and as such, contains information that might be stressful to the reader.

Please be aware that this book contains information, facts, statistics, and personal anecdotes about issues that include depression, anxiety, disordered eating, self-harm, and suicide. It contains content about personal experiences that include abuse and neglect, discrimination, death of loved ones, natural disasters, and other crises. Regardless of personal experience, this can be emotionally difficult material.

All the anecdotes in this book are from individuals currently in adolescence, or individuals describing their own experiences with stress and anxiety during their childhood and adolescence. Some of these anecdotes address how these individuals responded in a way that made their problems worse. Some of these anecdotes address what they wished they knew then, or how they wished they would have responded. In some cases, there is a positive resolution, and in some cases, the problem is ongoing.

The last few years have been a struggle. While these anecdotes are lightly edited for grammar and clarity, these stories come directly from adolescents who have experienced the real-life issues they're discussing. These anecdotes don't necessarily reveal perfect or ideal coping strategies. Life is messy and uncertain, and these vulnerable responses are honest reflections of that fact. I am grateful for the teens' willingness to be honest and let their stories be shared to benefit others.

Remember to care for your well-being and personal boundaries as you read. The sections in this book will contain clear information about the content. Self-care may mean taking breaks when needed, only reading some sections when prepared or comfortable to do so, or skipping some sections entirely.

The end of each chapter contains reflections and activity suggestions. These are designed to be moments of pause from the information presented in each chapter, especially because some of this reading might be upsetting or a lot to digest at once. Research shows that taking a "brain break" can reduce your stress and help you focus—in all of your daily tasks, from the classroom to at home. Even when our minds wander, as these activities ask us to do, our brains are at work behind the scenes processing. Pausing also helps our brains to recover so we can better focus later without distraction.[1] Take some time to rest between reading. Consider the ways we can use brain break habits in other aspects of our lives, as well.

And finally, you never have to experience crisis alone. If you are in distress, please refer to chapter 14, "Quick Guide to Resources." It contains many safe, confidential, free, immediate options available for you to talk, text, or chat with someone who can help.

If you are considering suicide or self-harm, call your emergency number or go to the emergency room immediately.

INTRODUCTION
STRESS AND THE PROBLEM WITH TIME

This introduction has been difficult for me to write because in many ways, words don't seem adequate to convey the way recent events have impacted global mental health.

Every year, the *Oxford English Dictionary* selects the "word of the year" that represents the year's overall mood and interests. For 2020, the makers of the dictionary announced they would pick multiple words because it had been such an "unprecedented" year. Those words included "COVID-19," "lockdown," and "Black Lives Matter." The word "pandemic" increased usage by 57,000%. Reflecting the drastic worldwide shift of multiple events, the language we used was in upheaval.[1] How do we cope with trauma, loss, and the unexpected when we're still inventing the words to communicate what we're experiencing?

Language can tell us a lot about how people live and function. Before the COVID-19 pandemic disrupted life as we knew it, the most used noun in the English language was "time."[2] It's true; we're obsessed with time.

Societally, our fixation on time—and how we use it—is reflected in the pressures that adolescents face from the adults who determine how we spend many of our hours. The schedule is filled for us in advance: we will attend school, do our homework and projects, get involved in extracurriculars or volunteer work, do our chores, get a job, and spend social time with family and friends. Plans for the school year and the holidays run on clear timetables. Furthermore, adolescence is filled with predictable plans for growth and milestones—what subjects we take in each grade, when we take standardized tests or sit for exams, when we learn to drive, and when we graduate. We make plans in adolescence for life after schooling is over—maybe college, career, or family—that sometimes embrace or clash with what our families and friends expect from us. Life is full of question marks that we've organized into timetables to better manage the uncertainty. In short, adolescence as a whole might be boiled down to a series of plans and goals with the assumption that time will flow forward as expected.

What happens when time stops? When the world grows chaotic and steals our normal clocks and calendars?

In recent years, society collectively learned a hard truth, one that individuals who struggle with mental and physical health conditions might already know all too well: plans are a privilege. The healthy and hopeful get to make and keep them. In 2020, our collective plans vanished into confusion as time ceased to follow a predictable path. Our schedules for school and work were thrown into chaos. Classrooms and work went remote or shut down completely. Our special events, gatherings, and holidays were canceled completely or reimagined in new forms, socially distanced or digital. Other events we were looking forward to would be rescheduled, deferred to some future time when things were safer.

Nobody knew when that would be. Soon, not soon? Who knew?

It is worth acknowledging that our societal love of time, plans, and action—that focus on turning uncertainty into schedules—made the COVID-19 pandemic and the questions it raised all the more stressful. Would we or our loved ones get sick, or even die? What would happen to our family members' jobs? Would we be going to school in person or remotely? Would remote school be easier, harder, or some strange combination of both? Would this educational change affect our future goals somehow? How long would we be behind face masks and digital screens? How would household relationships function under this pressure of being together all the time? Would healthy relationships stay healthy, and what would the terrible cost of abusive ones be?

We didn't know. We didn't have our normal schedule or priorities anymore—but suddenly our phones and emails and Zoom meetings filled our days with so many new digital tasks to learn and figure out in a short period of time. We didn't have the language to fully describe it, either, though we invented many new words to try to adapt. No wonder everyone was struggling—regardless of age. Uncertainty is hard. It is normal to feel destabilized when our routines and rituals become disrupted, to feel isolated when we have to withdraw from others. When we get to the point where we have to invent many entirely new words or begin using words that were never part of our daily vocabulary, we are experiencing something unprecedented. Experiencing crisis complicates caring for mental health. It is a fact worth acknowledging.

When the pandemic started, I was teaching high school seniors. One week I was in the classroom. The next week, I found myself online trying to invent new activities and lessons. I watched our normal calendar vanish: prom, all the special traditions and activity days, a traditional graduation. Many of my students were having a hard time being disconnected from everything. They didn't come to Zoom class or left their cameras off the whole time or didn't turn in their work. Who could blame them? I was stressed and upset too.

Meanwhile, some people were minimizing what teenagers were experiencing. One of my students, a graduating senior, wrote to me explaining why she'd been turning in late work. She was struggling with how her last year in high school was ending in a way she'd never expected, but her parents told her this difficulty was nothing. They said they had experienced much harder times in their lives. I could tell this made her feel even worse; there were a lot of apologies in the email. In response, I wrote back:

> I want you to know that it's okay to have those big feelings. You've lost memories you hoped for at special events you were excited to experience. You are learning how to learn in an unexpected new way that may not suit your abilities. Your stress about dorm life

and your college future is real. Do not feel the need to apologize for the stress you carry in a global crisis. I read a post online today from someone saying that when he was a senior in high school, some of his classmates were going off to the Vietnam War. His message was what adults always say to younger people to make them feel bad about themselves: "kids these days don't know what 'real' problems are."

This is an unacceptable thing to believe, much less say. There are no scales to weigh out wars and pandemics. Your problems are real. Even if others have had it worse. I want to state this clearly: just because others had a difficult experience doesn't mean your experiences aren't valid.

There is no point in comparing troubles—no one wins when stress and sorrow are a competition. It's not. You are not alone in feeling scared and overwhelmed. You are seen. It is okay to feel what you feel without shame or guilt.

Other students had immune disorders or immunosuppressed loved ones and lived under severe anxiety about their health. Some students simply couldn't focus at home working online and found it impossible to learn. Many of my students struggled with feeling isolated. None of them needed or deserved to hear their concerns be invalidated or undermined. All too often, adults can find it easy to dismiss adolescents, but the wide range of experiences and the stress accompanying them are valid.

For me, the pandemic affected my ability to communicate in a way I'd never anticipated at all. I was born with moderate hearing loss. It runs in the family; my mother and uncles are deaf. All our lives, we relied on reading lips to understand others. Hearing aids help, but they aren't enough without lipreading. When everyone began wearing masks, suddenly everyone's mouths disappeared and for those with hearing loss, the world became incredibly difficult to navigate.

In an ideal world where everyone's mouths were uncovered, it was already embarrassing for me to not understand people and ask them to repeat themselves constantly. In a pandemic world, it became *impossible* when I couldn't lipread, voices were distorted, and it was hard to determine who was speaking in a group of people. I have an unconscious habit of leaning in closer to hear better, which was mortifying when I realized I was inadvertently getting closer and making others uncomfortable while we were social distancing.

I've struggled for most of my life with social anxiety about communicating my hearing loss. The pandemic forced me to tell people over and over, "I'm sorry. I have hearing loss. Could you speak up? The mask makes it harder for me to hear you." Each time it felt stressful, but most people were understanding and helpful. I realized even people without hearing loss were struggling to make out people's voices. We *are* all in this together.

And so these strange times march on confusingly and with difficulty for all.

As I write this introduction, there is a chalkboard calendar hanging over my desk that claims it's March. It is not March. It's well past the month this calendar marked, March 2020—well over a year at this point. I didn't mean for this calendar to become a symbol for the way the pandemic hit the pause button on my life, but every time I thought about updating it to the current month—such a small task to erase a chalkboard and write in some new numbers—I felt exhausted. My stress response had been to do only the most essential tasks that I needed to function. Updating the calendar seemed like a waste of my personal energy. I didn't mean for the unmoving calendar to become a symbol of life on pause, but at some point, the unchanging calendar no longer measured days but something else that's hard to articulate—memories that didn't get made, places that didn't get visited, friends that didn't get hugged, plans that didn't become reality.

In retrospect, the stuck calendar reminds me of another period in my life where I was so stressed and frightened that I can barely recall what I did in that span of time. When I was twenty-one years old, Hurricane Katrina hit my hometown of New Orleans. For me personally, time seemed to stop for at least a year and a half. I'm sure for many others whose homes, families, and lives were catastrophically impacted, the "life on pause" feeling lasted even longer.

Like during the pandemic, I lived and breathed question marks. Where would we live, what would we do, when would everything feel okay again? I know that during that time period, I got up in the mornings, I had classes and a job, I had family and friends—but I remember close to nothing about it. Post-disaster left a blank space in the calendar of my life. This was a time that I surely must have survived *somehow*— because here I am—but I did not thrive. My life tasks were performed with my body sleepwalking while my mind checked out.

That feeling is very similar to what I have been feeling through the pandemic. That feeling is, quite simply, stress. We all experience stress, but it's highly likely that we are experiencing more of it than most of us have ever felt before, and it's been dragged out long-term.

Even putting aside losing my ability to easily lipread, it's been a long, hard, strange span of time for me. During the process of writing this book, so many stressful events derailed my progress. Perhaps this made the book all the better. I lived its subject matter as I wrote it. It's likely the stress of the year made me vulnerable to illness; I spent Thanksgiving 2020 intubated in the hospital's intensive care unit with pneumonia and pulmonary edema—a condition where the lungs fill up with fluid. Once I'd had that painful experience, I was all the more cautious and fearful that my respiratory system was vulnerable.

You probably know where this is going: seven months later, despite all precautions, I did catch a breakthrough case of COVID-19. Even after the worst symptoms were past, my brain was too foggy to write for a while.

One month after recovering from COVID-19, I had to evacuate my home after Hurricane Ida because I didn't have electricity for nearly two weeks. Though I was grateful to be spared major damage, it didn't help that it was Hurricane Katrina's anniversary as I sat in the dark and listened to the wind outside bring back an echo of past trauma. Ultimately, I can only hope that some of my own stressful experiences during the writing of this book can help you know that you are not alone and assist as you make meaning of your own hard times.

One piece of advice that we've all heard—part of our societal obsession with time, of course—is that *time heals everything*. I've never found this advice particularly useful! I think this advice comes from the desire to believe that there is a simple way to feel better, and it just comes from waiting. While it's true that some stressful things can be forgotten as they fade into the past, and that creating distance from certain people and events is necessary to process and heal, time isn't a cure-all. The scars of some abuses, losses, and trauma can return again and again. Grief isn't linear, and thinking it is "past" just means that when it erupts again, it can be even more disruptive and traumatic when it takes us by surprise.

When we praise time as the ultimate cure, we run the risk of forgetting and repeating the past's mistakes—both in personal ways and in larger cultural ways, especially when it comes to racism, sexism, and other social afflictions. The pandemic is a reminder in some ways that time doesn't always move normally, and in those circumstances, this advice can hinder rather than help. The past doesn't always fall away from us when we're limited in where we can go, who we can see, and what we can do. When that limited list of who we can see is a toxic or abusive list, time doesn't move at all. When that limited list of what we can do doesn't include the things that feed our coping and healing abilities, time doesn't move either. And when we don't know when a circumstance will end or improve, how can we live with the stress it brings us?

There are tools that can help us. This book addresses the role our minds and bodies play in our health and ability to cope with any difficulties we encounter. Even if nothing else in our life changes, when we understand better why our minds and bodies behave as they do, stress becomes easier to manage. Understanding can unlock some of stress's locked doors that lead to ineffective habits.

When stress becomes easier to manage, we can make better choices and build more effective life habits for ourselves. Maybe even more importantly, understanding stress can help us contextualize our choices and eventually forgive ourselves for making poor choices under pressure. All of these things can lead to better mental health. That is my hope for you.

ACTIVITY BREAK: REFLECTING ON TIME

What if you could reinvent your typical schedule and life goals, both long term and short term? What would your ideal major life milestones and events be—what would you keep, and what would you change? (Would you swap prom for something else? Is there something you like better than marking a sixteenth or eighteenth birthday?) Would you want more or less structure in your days for school or work? What about the start times and end times? What would your best working hours be (how do you function in morning, afternoon, and night, and what kind of breaks do you need)? Would you prefer year-round schooling where the 180 days are spread across the year (for example, with four 45-day school sessions split by two-week breaks, or with three 60-day school sessions split by twenty-day breaks)? Or would you prefer the nine-month academic calendar with a three-month summer break? Take some time to think about time.

PART I

WHAT IS STRESS?

CHAPTER ONE

EXPLORING STRESS

WHAT IS STRESS?

On some level, we all know what stress is—no one is fully immune to the body's response to physical, mental, or emotional experiences. Every living creature, human and non-human alike, has a response to internal and external issues. That response is called *stress*, and those issues are called *stressors*. In short, stressors trigger stress, which is how our body regulates itself when faced with change, danger, or even exciting challenges and accomplishments.

The medical definition of stress is "[a] psychophysiological response to real or perceived pressures in the environment."[1] The word "pressure" is deliberately vague because a wide variety of things can move us, not only what we consider "negative" experiences. Stress responses include hormonal changes and automatic adjustments to our brain function, breath rate, heartbeat, digestion, and many other physiological and mental processes. This means stress produces an observable, measurable impact on both our mental and physical states. Stress does not exist solely "in our heads"—the mind and body are intimately connected. It alters how we process our thoughts and emotions. It alters how we exist in our bodies and respond to our surroundings.

The stress response evolved to keep our bodies in a state of awareness and tension for when we need to act. In short, stress responses are survival adaptations. Yes, having stress is an evolutionary advantage! Our bodies are programmed to ensure we live through dangerous new experiences, changing situations, and demanding tasks. Because it is a developmental period marked by many changes, stressors occur more frequently during adolescence than at other times in our lives.[2]

However, when we talk about "feeling stressed," generally we mean that we feel overwhelmed by or not equipped to cope with our experiences. Stress has a negative reputation because stress responses emerge specifically in those times of change, pressure, or danger—that is, times we associate generally with negativity. Furthermore, the mental and physical sensations that our stress responses provoke can feel profoundly unpleasant, the opposite of helpful. However, the way we think about and talk about stress can strongly impact how we experience it. If we think about having stress as only negative, stress becomes that much more difficult to bear.

Stress is not the same as *distress*. These are two different things. That's why it's important to clarify that stress itself is not unhealthy, though we tend to talk about it like it is. Stress can be motivating or inspiring. Many people work best under some form of moderate stress pushing them to work faster, looser, more creatively. Normal levels of stress can enhance alertness, improve the memory, and help us learn under pressure.[3]

During difficult times, our bodies are in survival mode, fighting for our benefit. It is not uncommon to think that at times our bodies seem to be deliberately working *against* us and our needs. We've probably felt this way many times. And yet our bodies have carried us through so much. They carry us every step of the way, through stressors big and small—through homework and humiliations, natural disasters and heartbreak, personal suffering and losing loved ones, and still they carry on. Have we frozen up in some stressful moments, unable to act or think? Yes. Have we gotten physically ill during and after stressful times? Yes. Have we experienced mental and physical states that caused us pain and suffering? Yes. But our bodies keep on going, trying to pull us through those moments to the other side, however imperfectly.

If stress itself is normal—and even an evolutionary advantage—then why does this book exist? Excessive or constant stress over periods of time can be harmful, "contribut[ing] to hormonal imbalances, lowered immune system function, and increased susceptibility to disease."[4] However, if we can better understand how stress works and the ways it can be effective, we can destigmatize some of its reputation and lessen its burden when we experience it. Furthermore, by understanding its function and the process behind it, we can make its inevitable occurrence less painful for ourselves while increasing tolerance for serious or extended stress.

HOW DO STRESS RESPONSES WORK?

Stress can seem mystifying when everyone is affected by similar circumstances in very different ways. If we all have stress responses, how can some people move through life seeming unbothered by something that might devastate another? Let's begin by looking at stress on a very basic level to clarify the changes that take place in the body and brain when we're stressed, as well as why they occur.

Stress's physiological and psychological effects "are meant to enhance the likelihood of survival."[5] Our brains monitor for stressors by surveying our external surroundings and our internal states to ensure

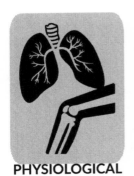  

PHYSIOLOGICAL   **NEUROLOGICAL**   **PSYCHOLOGICAL**

Effects related to our nervous system that controls our body—which includes the brain, spinal cord, and nerves—are referred to as neurological. Effects related to our bodily functions are referred to as physiological. Effects related to our mental and emotional states are referred to as psychological. Stress is a neurological function that affects your physiological and psychological state. *Illustration by Christie Cognevich.*

there are no concerns and to check for any changes taking place. The brain interprets "change" as "potential for danger," so it is especially alert and sensitive to new experiences, transitions, and uncertainties. Furthermore, while humans are flexible creatures, it appears that there is a limit to the amount of change and newness that human beings can endure easily without distress.[6] This is why any "first" experience— starting a new grade or transitioning to a new school, moving to a new house or starting over in a new city, a first kiss—is often stressful for us. It's coded into our neurological wiring.

If the brain notices a potential challenge—whether inside or outside the body—we call this a *stressor*. Because adolescence is an identity-forming time in which our brains and bodies transition from childhood to adulthood, there are many pressures we might face along the way. Common adolescent stressors include:

- Academic concerns, including grades, future college/career decisions, and juggling societal, family, and personal expectations and pressure

- Social relationships, including fitting in, peer pressure, friendship, dating, and sexuality

- Family relationships, including household dynamics, stability, and finances

- Body image, including physical development and pressure to fit social norms

- Time management, including school/work/life balance and time for sleep[7]

This is just a general list of stressors. Stressors vary, and can range from a loud or annoying noise to a broken leg. Anything that we find challenging or important enough to provoke a reaction—whether it causes worry, annoyance, or even excitement and joy—can be a stressor.

TODAY'S DATE

9/23

TODAY'S POTENTIAL STRESSORS

chemistry test
turning in English project
seeing L on Friday
work schedule

MAJOR TASKS

-proofread English project at lunch and submit before 5th period
-remind mom to book dentist appt.
-ask off work 10/3—don't forget

MINOR TASKS

-check agenda for next week's schedule
-history reading—p. 97

-make terms Quizlet with S for Wed.
return library books
-text L

JOYS

Fall is here. Looking forward to October & decorating the house for Halloween. Love the weather when I'm walking the dogs.

SORROWS

Early sunsets make me tired and feeling down sometimes. Things aren't going like I thought they would with L. Hard to focus on chemistry when I'm worried about work and L instead.

Stressor trackers like this one can help determine potential triggers and patterns in your activities, interactions, and emotions. Download a free blank version from the author's website at christiecognevich.com. *Illustration by Christie Cognevich.*

In response to the stressor, the brain sends hormonal signals to the rest of the body to prepare it for action. What action our bodies prepare for will depend on what our brains determine will help us survive the situation: fighting, running away, going still, or turning to another individual or a community for help. The brain's decision-making and signal-sending all occur quickly and unconsciously.

There are multiple processes that take place at this point, but we will focus first on the physiological effect known as the *fight-or-flight response*. This stress response causes many major, complex changes in the human body's standard functions. Every system and organ uses energy to perform tasks. In general, the stress response rearranges our energy reserves, prioritizing oxygen and nutrients to feed organs that serve the immediate moment's needs. Long-term processes like digestion and immune system function are halted or slowed in favor of short-term processes to help us escape the stressor. For example, stress responses increase oxygen-rich blood flow to our brains to enhance our ability to sense, process, and react to new information. Blood flow also increases to our muscles, which tense up to aid faster action and movement.

The fight-or-flight response affects the body in many ways, and some of these sensations might be familiar. Each of these physiological changes has a purpose, but can cause discomfort:

- The heartbeat speeds up and blood pressure rises so that blood cells can deliver nutrients and oxygen to the rest of the body quicker. This can feel like a racing heartbeat or abnormal pulse.

- Similarly, the breath rate increases to get more oxygen into the bloodstream. This can feel like shortness of breath, and rapid, shallow breaths can trigger panic attacks.

- The stomach and intestines slow their processes. This can lead to a fluttery or nervous feeling in the stomach. Decreased production of a mucus protecting the stomach lining from acid can lead to heartburn or stomachaches.

- Overall, any organs or processes not essential to immediate survival receive less blood and nutrients—for example, our extremities like the toes and fingers might feel cold or tingly because of decreased blood flow.[8]

There are many other changes, but these are the ones most likely to sound familiar. Remember, this is a broad and general list of physiological changes triggered by a fight-or-flight stress response; not everyone's experiences will be identical, and not every stressor causes identical symptoms.

Not all stress responses are designed for actions like fighting and fleeing. Another stress response deals with social action. The impulse to affiliate with others in stressful times is known as the *tend-and-befriend* response. Because we lack "thick skin, sharp teeth, quick reflexes, [and] camouflage to protect [our]selves, human beings have adopted group living as the primary solution to problems of survival and reproduction."[9] Why might the brain choose this response? The clearest evolutionary advantage of social bonding is that larger groups are more likely to have the resources and knowledge to address threats. Ultimately, there are also mental and physical health reasons behind the brain's stressed impulse to seek support from community, a friend, or a pet: social bonds are essential to both human development and our continued well-being. We have learned that infants need both nutritional sustenance *and* affection from their caregivers in order to thrive. Lack of nurturing contact from caregivers has been proven to cause developmental disorders and even death.[10] Even once grown, socially isolated individuals report higher rates of health disorders than individuals with social support systems.[11]

Like the fight-or-flight response, there is a neurological component to our urges to seek out companionship or support from others. Social bonding is encouraged by the release of oxytocin, a hormone associated strongly with love, social affection, and pain relief. Oxytocin's "primary effects appear to be the enhancement of empathy and of deep emotional bonds" between individuals, as well as improving "the body's ability to heal itself."[12] It helps us feel safe, calm, and improves our immune system. Oxytocin also aids in bonding between humans and animals, enhancing the therapeutic effect of emotional support animals. Successfully fulfilling our social needs can provide a tremendous sense of relief and well-being stimulated through the release of more oxytocin.

As we can see, humans need these stress responses. They keep our inner state and outer reality in touch with each other. In fact, studies have shown that animals lacking stress responses cannot survive without special care from others to ensure they live.[13] If humans never had stress, we would be much more likely to have many serious accidents leading to injuries and deaths. Our sharpened instincts and ability to respond to a danger have saved us more times than we probably realize. Stress assists us in developing new skills during critical moments—when we're at the edge of our knowledge and comfort zones, stress can push us to make an intuitive leap and try new ideas. On a subconscious level, our brains sense subtle danger signs in our environments and regularly work to help us.

When we swerve and brake to avoid hitting a dog running across the road, stress equipped us to make that spur-of-the-moment decision in a pinch—we mentally processed the danger, then physically reacted as needed. When we reach out to our best friends or feel the need to go home to our family and pets, our body is signaling a need for the healing that oxytocin, stimulated by social contact, offers us. Our brains notice things—a speeding car, for example—and acts on them, giving us a burst of speed to get out of the way before we realize consciously that there is a problem at all. "I didn't even see that car coming," we might think to ourselves as we reach the other side just in time to feel the car rush by in a blur of motion. Most likely, our brains processed subconsciously some subtle environmental shift, like hearing engine noise close by. Fear and discomfort can be beneficial, motivating us to confide in a family member or friend so that we can avoid a dangerous person, choice, or situation. Getting the sense that someone is giving off "bad vibes" is really our stress response attuned to subtle danger cues.

Our stress responses deliver gut instincts and can be thanked when surviving "near-miss" close calls.

WHY DO STRESS RESPONSES VARY?

Stress responses depend on the person and situation. Though we all experience stress, our individual experiences can diverge tremendously—not everyone experiences the same stressors or stress responses. It all depends on the issue itself, our surroundings, genetic makeup, social conditions, as well as other interconnected factors. Some threats might cause the heartbeat to slow instead of accelerate. Some experiences might stress one person, but leave another unbothered. Just as every illness has different symptoms and the immune system response affects individuals differently, think of the stress response as variable.

Our early life experiences can shape how we respond to stressors. Studies show that greater levels of stress in our early life can make us more vulnerable to stressful environments. We know that individuals exposed to traumatic events tend to have increased levels of stress hormones when encountering stressors, even ones unrelated to prior trauma.[14] Someone who has been abused might process a family dinner as a highly stressful event; someone who has had a healthy and fulfilling family life might not understand what a terrifying and daunting task it might be to sit at a dinner table with others.

Furthermore, the level of control we believe we have over the stressor affects how it impacts us. Excellent students might still find test-taking to be a high-pressure situation, especially if they feel like there are factors out of their control impacting their academic performance. Those more invested in sports might be unbothered by test-taking, but find the intense scrutiny of the coach or other teammates to be difficult. And regardless of our values and priorities, many individuals work well under certain amounts of pressure.

Also, stress can vary because we don't recognize it, especially in moments we consider positive or exciting. Remember that stressors can't necessarily be categorized as "good" or "bad." Anything that is potentially challenging, important, or moves us to reaction is a possible stressor, not only "bad" experiences. Notice how the physical stress response described previously can fit a moment of delight or exhilaration also: finding out we're going on a trip to Disney World, kissing someone we really like for the first time, doing well at tryouts for a sports team. Our breathing shifts, our heartbeats race, our bodies tingle. Sometimes we are experiencing stress without knowing it. Unhappiness, pain, and discomfort aren't the sole emotional states for being stressed. Pure joy can be overwhelming or lead to nerves and uncertainty.

Additionally, because there are multiple pathways through our body sending information and nutrients, sometimes we delayed stress responses. The electrical signals sent by our brain through the nervous system can help us duck a rock thrown at us with only seconds to process it. However, other nutrients and hormonal signals travel via the bloodstream; the circulatory system pumps those along slower than those lightning-fast neurological messages. This results in some symptoms of our stress response occurring minutes later. We might not realize why we feel worked up because the stressor has already passed.[15]

The nature of our stress responses and our ability to function under pressure isn't a verdict on our personal qualities—the severity or type of stress response is unrelated to strength or bravery. Stress responses depend on a number of complicated genetic and environmental factors. For example, our blood pressure might rise more (hypertension) because of a genetic predisposition to cardiovascular reactions. Having parents with hypertension might make our circulatory system more reactive to stressors. The unconscious impulse for fight-or-flight, tend-and-befriend, and other responses is similarly varied. For example, the tend-and-befriend response is not exclusive to extroverts; even introverts can experience the desire to have friends, family, or pets to accompany them in stressful situations.

While some of our stress responses are inherited from our genes, others are based on social histories and learned behaviors; whether inherited or learned, the brain's impulses aren't always the most effectively

MY WEEK IN REVIEW

SUMMARY

Had an awesome week of basketball practices, and we won against MHS. Dad and K came to the game for the first time. Really excited for next week, vs. LHS. School was okay. A lot of homework, nothing much to say about class.

SELF-EVALUATION

SLEEP
Been sleeping maybe 6 hours a night. Not great. Need more before games, definitely.

SOCIAL
Practice days are always pretty social. Saw a movie with K on Sunday. Feeling good about social stuff.

WATER
64 oz. water per day daily, except for Friday when I did only 55 oz. No coffee since last week!

SCHOOL/WORK
Just okay. Got a B- on anatomy quiz, B+ on the Macbeth quiz.

MOVEMENT
Next week we only have one day of practice; need to take some walks on off days.

PERSONAL
I really like K. She's been great about my practice schedule. Want to take her out next week.

Because stress varies from day to day, and some stress responses can fly under the radar, weekly trackers like this one reveal patterns in our activities, interactions, and self-care. Trackers can help reveal ongoing issues, effective or ineffective habits, and/or show our improved self-care over time. Download a free blank version from the author's website at christiecognevich.com. *Illustration by Christie Cognevich.*

suited to the moment.[16] If we lost a loved one in a car accident, we might be stressed to the point of terror by the prospect of learning how to drive—we might freeze up or want to avoid the situation completely. Or, alternatively, we might be fueled by aggression, and in response, feel the impulse to drive too fast and take risks. Others might be motivated to drive only with a trusted loved one and never alone. The brain does its best to evaluate situations in rapid speed under pressure, which means it can sometimes choose ineffective options. Furthermore, there aren't always clear-cut links we can trace between our stressors and responses. Bodies and brains are complex; a stress response should not be a judgment about our personal qualities.

While having stress is involuntary, we still have choice over our actions in the end. Our brains prepare and encourage our bodies to act, but we don't *have* to fight or flee or seek out someone else. We can decide to ignore our desire to yell or fight, or dismiss the urge to call a friend, if these are ineffective ways to handle the issue. With practice, it gets easier to identify when we're experiencing stress, what actions that stress response is urging, and weigh whether it serves our needs before acting.

Finally, the manner in which we respond to a stressor isn't permanent. Our brains are always learning new habits and are capable of responding differently in the future. We can change ineffective habits and learn new ones.

What types of experiences or environments do you find the most stressful?

Matt

I have mild autism and social anxiety, so anything with social interaction stresses me out, to be honest. Family, friends, strangers, it doesn't matter. Just thinking about people talking to me or looking at me makes me want to curl up on the floor. I don't know why. It started getting worse when I was eleven or twelve, around then. Familiar environments are fine. It's just when I'm out of my comfort zone that I struggle.

I guess I should say it's not that I'm always stressed talking to everyone in any circumstance. It's social interaction where I'm not completely comfortable with all the people and the place we're at. Like, I can have dinner with my immediate family at home and it's usually good. But holiday dinners with extended family where there's all the cousins and everyone's asking you questions about what you've been up to? I can't do it. I'll literally get dizzy and can't breathe.

When the pandemic started and people started wearing masks, it's the same thing. They look unfamiliar, I panic and freeze up.

Luckily my parents understand, so I'm allowed to stay home from any events I'm not comfortable with. My dad's side of the family is pretty cool about it. I see my grandparents when it's smaller and quieter, and they come over to our house where I'm more comfortable. We have a good relationship. Some of my mom's side of the family thinks I'm a spoiled brat, though. I tried to go to their big family Christmas last year to make my grandma happy because every year and every holiday she's upset about me not coming, but I ended up throwing up and was sick the whole time. It was just a nightmare.

It used to be that classrooms were the worst for me because I had so much anxiety about not knowing if I'd be called on. I couldn't look up and make eye contact with anyone. I would just be sweating, literally, dreading having to talk to people.

After I had a panic attack in history class over it, I got a formal diagnosis of social anxiety disorder. I remember sitting at my desk just thinking, *please don't call on me, please don't call on me*, over and over. I knew the answer, I just couldn't handle everyone looking at me while I answered if she called on me. And of course, she called on me. It was like there was a zipper in my chest that someone zipped closed and squeezed all the air out of me.

After that happened and I got diagnosed, now the school counselor notifies all my teachers about my social anxiety every year. Basically, one of my accommodations is that teachers won't

Matt's mild autism became increasingly difficult for him during the pandemic, with face masks making people look unfamiliar to him. Even though he knows most of the people in his class, he struggles with making eye contact and talking to people. *Illustration by Kate Haberer.*

call on me randomly. I can volunteer when my anxiety is low and I'm feeling good. Having control of it—knowing that I can raise my hand when I'm ready to handle attention—really helps. I think I'm more focused in class, too, because I can listen instead of just thinking *please don't call on me* the whole time.

Going to school online has made some of that anxiety come back. I feel weird being on camera. It's the same uncomfortable feeling I get when there are eyes on me in person because I can't really tell who's looking at me when we're all on Zoom. That has been a real struggle, especially since teachers have asked us to leave our cameras on so they can see we're here and we're working. I haven't figured out how to handle it yet, really.

Bella

I'm a nervous wreck taking tests in math. I'm in all honors and Advanced Placement classes in my other subjects, but math is nothing but a ball of anxiety for me. I have dyscalculia, which is basically like math dyslexia, a learning disorder with numbers. It's hard to explain. It's not that I can't do math problems at all, it just takes me a really long time to process it all out because something about numbers just doesn't click in my head like words do.

I need something to touch or help me visualize numbers because mental math is so hard for me. When I was in first grade, my teacher showed me how to draw dots on the numbers and then tap on them to help me count. I couldn't add up numbers without drawing the dots and tapping them. Even though I don't have to draw the dots anymore, now that I've been doing it for years, I can visualize the dot points and I still tap them. I definitely use my fingers to count still because numbers are so weird for me that I need something solid to make them real.

That means I'm just really slow at math, so tests are really stressful for me. Especially standardized tests. It's embarrassing to be tapping on my paper or drawing tally marks or using my fingers like a little kid when I'm in high school. I will say it's gotten a *lot* better at higher level math where we're allowed to use calculators, but there are still some things we're expected to memorize that just don't make sense to me when it comes to numbers.

Leila

My old high school was a huge source of stress. I went to a school that was not diverse at all, so I was never comfortable there. I didn't fit in, but I wasn't afraid to tell people what I thought or respond when they'd said something racist. One girl flat out told me racism "wasn't real" and just something minorities made up to feel sorry for themselves.

My first year there, the administrator in charge of scheduling refused to put me in any honors classes except Spanish. She told me the only reason I was in honors for Spanish was because it was my "native language." I'm very proud of my heritage, but that doesn't change that I was born in the United States and English is my first language. She just assumed that I spoke Spanish as a first language.

It was a terrible environment for me, and I felt it like a weight on my chest every day I was there.

Amelia

My house is such a stressful place. It's always been really chaotic—I live with my dad, stepmom, grandparents, and a bunch of step-siblings and half-siblings depending on what day it is—but it's gotten worse during the pandemic. When there's too many people and too much chaos, I just can't relax. They're all just big personalities. It's a *lot* to take in. You never know who's going to be home and who's fighting and so on.

School was kind of my escape from the crazy home life. When we had to do virtual learning, I lost being able to go to school and be somewhere I can focus. Even though I was in class I'd have to turn off the camera and make lunch for my sister or help everyone else do their schoolwork. I could barely get anything done. I don't even have a word for how hard—maybe "ordeal." It's been an ordeal.

Some of my friends were annoyed about going back to in-person school, but not me. Honestly, I could not wait to get out of the house again.

John

I think any competitive environment where I feel insecure chips away at me. I know I'm a hard worker, but some people are effortlessly smart. I'm not. I'd like to think that pressure makes me work harder and better, but it doesn't. It just makes me question myself more. I work better in just a regular old classroom where everyone and everything is average.

Growing up, I really wanted to be a surgeon. I knew it was going to be a lot of work, but that was the dream. I was lucky enough to get into this summer program for high schoolers who were interested in the medical profession, and I immediately felt out of place. Just instant—everyone else looked so *smart*.

They gave us these white lab coats, which I loved wearing, but I didn't actually enjoy the lab experiences we did. There were supposed to be cool activities like stitching sutures on an orange. Everyone else was so good at it, with the thread neat and straight. They were all comparing each other's work and trying to decide which one looked best. It wasn't me, that's for sure. I'm left-handed, and my stitches looked terrible.

I didn't really make any friends in the program, and I don't know if I wasn't very friendly because I was insecure, or what, but that was hard too. In the end, I finished the program feeling like at least I found out that it wasn't really for me before I went to college and not when I was in a pre-med program or even in med school.

Left-handed John struggles with the activities at a summer medical internship. He thought he wanted to be a surgeon, but the experience only made him feel out of place and unhappy. *Illustration by Kate Haberer.*

What do you need most when you're stressed? What kind of environment or help from others do you need?

Leila

I need a clean area to work in. If it's not clean, it's distracting. When my bedroom is messy or cluttered, I can't even think. I hate classrooms where there's just junk in boxes everywhere and the teacher's desk looks like a tornado hit it.

When I'm too worked up to think, I'll just clean. Do the laundry, rearrange my room, whatever. Maybe I'm procrastinating a little, but I need it! I can get a lot more done after I've cleaned.

Bella

Mostly, I need space to be left alone. My girlfriend, Em, is amazing in almost every way, but she's the opposite, so she has a hard time with this. When she's upset or anxious, she needs someone nearby. The more people the better. Em relaxes when she's got lots of people to talk to.

Our first fight was about that, actually. Almost a year ago, I think. I forgot what I was upset about—something about school—but I told Em I didn't want to talk, which hurt her feelings. At first, we had a pretty hard time getting what each other needed, but it's gotten better.

I'm an introvert. Having to talk about it before I'm ready to talk is horrible. I need a little alone time to think and chill out. Now I tell her, "I'm not ready to talk yet, but I'll call you later," or something like that, instead of "I don't want to talk about it." The phrasing matters to her, and I get that. One just shuts her down, the other lets her know I'll be there when I'm ready.

Also, since I got a car, it's gotten a lot easier for me to cope with stress. I'll just go for a drive and turn the music up while I drive around and think. Not even for that long, maybe just fifteen or twenty minutes. That helps me unwind.

ACTIVITY BREAK: MENTAL VACATIONS

When it's impossible or not useful to step away from a moment physically, we can still take mental vacations.

Take some time to design an interesting mental getaway you would enjoy, realistic or not. What types of locations do you find soothing? Would you go to the beach, a rose garden, or outer space? What time of day would you go—do you like dawn or sunset, the brilliant sunshine of daytime, the deep dark of night, or some combination of light and dark, like the shade of trees or the bright neon lights of a city at night? What sounds would fill your vacation? Waves crashing, or wind rustling leaves? Scents, tastes, textures? Wander through a dream vacation for ten minutes. Try to engage all five senses, though this can be tricky.

It isn't effective to always be in a difficult moment, just as it isn't effective to always be checked out. Mental vacations require balance. It might be hard to "check out" and "check in" again when you're done, but with practice, we can help our brains take some time away *and* return back to the present moment a little easier.

CHAPTER TWO

EXPERIENCING LONG-TERM STRESS IN A CHAOTIC WORLD

VULNERABILITY IN AN ERA OF CHANGE

Technological change produces social and cultural change. For the vast majority, life without our phones, apps, and the internet would be unthinkable. As a result, we live in a chaotic, sometimes overwhelming world where media and technology make life easier and harder at the same time. Nearly *all* American teenagers have smartphones or access to one; nearly half describe themselves as online "almost constantly."[1] Information fills our screens faster than we can process it. The COVID-19 pandemic added an additional layer of complication to our already full online lives; undoubtedly, the percentage of teenagers describing themselves as online "almost constantly" would go up much higher because of our worldwide, intense reliance on the internet for school, work, and socializing.

In chapter 1, we noted that there is a limit to the amount of change and newness humans can experience without distress. The sheer volume of information available to us online, and how quickly that grows and changes on a daily basis (and even more accurately, a second-by-second basis as we can refresh and see new updates constantly), is itself a stressor, even if it is also fulfilling. It's likely that our older family members had access to a library, the local newspaper, and the nightly news growing up, and these represent a vanishing fraction of data we have flying at us from our multiple screens. People study in school for future jobs that may not yet exist for a technology that hasn't been invented yet. In fact, in 2010, the top ten jobs in the United States hadn't even existed in the six years prior.[2]

Fear of missing out is common. Amid the landslide of information and images, society presents its version of beauty, success—even how to struggle, but still look good and stay positive while overcoming ordeals. Even tears can become glamorized with the right filters. The pressure to look and behave a certain way comes at us from all directions, in person and online. Remember the medical definition of stress from chapter 1? Stress is our "response to real or perceived pressures in the environment."[3] That pressure can be everywhere in this era.

After all, how can we stand out in a world with nearly eight billion other humans?

We've all heard the common criticism that our media-saturated culture promotes self-obsession. Social work professor and researcher Brené Brown points out that when we consider our narcissistic traits in a softer human light, they look different: "I see the shame-based fear of being ordinary. I see the fear of never feeling extraordinary enough to be noticed, to be lovable, to belong, or to cultivate a sense of purpose."[4] Far from a sense of inflated self-worth, Brown suggests that many of us share a fear of what we *lack*. Those who "grow up on a steady diet of reality television, celebrity culture, and unsupervised social media can absorb this messaging and develop a completely skewed sense of the world. *I am only as good as the number of 'likes' I get on Facebook or Instagram.*"[5] After all, it is all too easy for us to fill in the phrase "*never _____ enough.*"[6] What would we write in that space? How many words rise to mind immediately? Good, strong, pretty, thin, smart, talented, popular, influential, belonging, loved?

Ultimately, we are in an age where what we *lack* seems profound. Even before the COVID-19 pandemic, Brown writes, "From 9/11, multiple wars, and the recession, to catastrophic natural disasters and the increase in random violence and school shootings, we've survived and are surviving events that have torn at our sense of safety with such force that we've experienced them as trauma even if we weren't directly involved."[7] This painful sense of emptiness, the blank space, the lack, leads us to compare what we have (and don't have) to everyone else. That mindset spreads across communities, into schools, families, our own minds. We compare, feel hungry, ashamed, invisible, and disconnected, struggling to be seen and heard in the crowd.

Understanding and support can be hard to come by. The adolescent challenges of earlier generations were different. For many teens, the adults in their lives aren't familiar with the same joys and sorrows of having a digital youth. All too often they can invalidate our experiences by referencing those aforementioned "narcissistic" tendencies. Sometimes they only reference the benefits of growing up in the present day ("you have it so much easier than I did!") while at the same time suggesting that any downsides are the fault of the younger generation themselves and not the unique problems we face ("kids these days!"). If we do have understanding adult support systems in our lives, even they may not always be able to offer strategies that fit our current lived experiences because they did not grow up with the same issues. These misunderstandings, invalidations, and missing guidance can be enormous stressors in themselves.

As a result, an ever-growing number of adolescents struggle with anxiety and depression. Even before the pandemic began, reports showed teenagers struggling over very real concerns about violence, climate change, and poverty, among other stressors. For example, in 2016, 12.8 percent of youths ages twelve to seventeen reported experiencing a major depressive episode in the past year, a steady increase of nearly 5 percent over a period of six years.[8] Nearly a third of American teenagers (32 percent) have experienced an anxiety disorder (which includes general anxiety, social anxiety, panic attacks, and post-traumatic stress disorder, among others) during their lifetime. Over 8 percent had an anxiety disorder categorized as "severe impairment."[9]

We are still learning how the COVID-19 pandemic will affect our mental health in the long run. The Centers for Disease Control and Prevention (CDC) noted in 2020 that early findings show the pandemic has prompted some mental health crises in adolescents experiencing school closures and the social isolation that goes along with it.[10] According to the Child Mind Institute, the 2020 Coronavirus Health and Impact Survey revealed that about 70 percent of both children and adults reported some degree of mental discomfort causing loneliness, irritability, or restlessness and fidgeting, and more than half of those under age seventeen reported feeling more sad, depressed, or unhappy as a result of their lives being disrupted.[11] The Morgan Stanley Alliance for Children's Mental Health survey conducted in summer 2021 revealed that while a smaller percentage of teenagers said the downtime of the pandemic improved their mental health, 37 percent said it worsened their mental health.[12] Almost half of all teenagers surveyed indicated concern about experiencing social anxiety when returning to regular activities (48 percent) and falling behind academically (47 percent).[13]

But not everyone has been equally impacted. Recent studies in 2021 show the pandemic has had very different impacts on different populations. We are seeing negative mental health effects on vulnerable populations, including BIPOC and LGBTQ+ adolescents, teens with unstable homes, and those experiencing anxiety, depression, ADHD, autism, and learning disorders. Those who live in stable homes that did not experience job or income loss appear to have been the most resilient. Adolescents in this category experienced the least negative mental health outcomes, or bounced back quickly after initial anxiety over the pandemic. Ultimately, adolescents appear to be strongly affected by how stressed their parents were and how they saw their parents coping during the pandemic.[14]

These findings tells us that if we have strong family ties, financial security, and healthy social support, the tend-and-befriend stress response works well. However, those of us who lack wealth, resources, and stable families might need additional support. For many, schools were a place to get hot meals, socialize in a healthy way, pursue studies to break cycles of poverty and abuse, and enjoy extracurricular activities in an environment safer than the streets or home. Even for those not interested in academics, school as a physical location could serve as an escape. Losing that can prompt extreme distress, or even a low-level but long-lasting stress that chips away at our resilience. Even as many students return to school in person, new restrictions and changes can be ongoingly stressful. However, the good news is that humans are resilient. Two-thirds of teenagers feel hopeful that they will adapt and rebound from the pandemic.[15]

This chapter containing information about why and when stress becomes unhealthy isn't meant to be alarming, though it may contain some concerning details about the effects of long-term stress. Remember that having stress is normal and part of every healthy human life. The knowledge of how and why stress can cause negative health outcomes can provide us with clarity when we experience it. There are reasons for how our bodies function (and how this can go wrong) that we can identify. Understanding the ways in which these processes go wrong can be an incredibly helpful first step to coping in difficult circumstances.

WHEN DOES STRESS BECOME UNHEALTHY?

In the previous chapter, we established that stress is necessary. If stress is so essential to our survival, why do we worry about having it? The term "stress" originated from the engineering term referring to any force applied to a material.[16] If that material is changed in some way by that force—deformed, bent, or moved—the result is called "strain." Our stress is similar to the engineering version; if our bodies experience pressure for too long, we become strained. Long-term stress, known as *chronic stress*, can take a serious toll on our mental and physical health. In short, stress is normal; chronic stress is not. Stress is not a disorder, but chronic stress can lead to mental and physical health disorders.

We can bounce back from a rough day at school, a fight with a friend, a sarcastic comment online, or a tense mealtime arguing with family. But bad day after bad day, tense night after tense night, if the situation doesn't improve, we become strained.

For most of human history, we spent most of our time hunting, gathering, and seeking shelter from predators and the elements. Stress's psychological and physiological changes (under the fight-or-flight response in particular) evolved as adaptations for short-term, immediate moments. Once we have acted on and survived a challenge, our bodies need to return to normal and rest.[17] At the time our stress responses evolved, humanity's survival problems were largely physical, immediate life-or-death threats requiring quick bursts of energy to fight or run. A hunter-gatherer society might encounter sudden hazards like dangerous animals and harsh weather, but there were no constant deadlines and tests and colleges.

The primary long-term stressor early humans faced was food shortages. Our stress response that evolved to cope with this was the increased production of the stress hormone cortisol. When we're facing starvation, cortisol works ideally: it increases blood sugar, which provides a brain boost when our energy is low (think of it working like an energy shot, a quick sugar high). It also slows growth and reproductive abilities.[18] This makes sense when the long-term stressor is a food shortage. The blood sugar spike helps energize us to think and hunt when we might be weaker than normal. When the long-term stressor *isn't* a food shortage, that increased cortisol doesn't help us survive or thrive. It does the opposite—leaving us with unhealthy bodily changes that affect our development and can lead to disorder and disease.

However, modern human concerns have changed from early history, while the stress responses haven't kept up the pace of change. Our stressors are often more emotional than physical in nature and of much longer duration. When our fight-or-flight response is triggered, it may not be appropriate or effective. Unfortunately, many modern problems don't tend to be improved by physical action like punching someone or by escaping (figuratively or literally). Preparing for a physical response won't help us respond to someone's cruel online comment. Even stressors related to our physical survival, such as living with an abusive or neglectful family, tend to require more emotional coping skills and social resources than physical skills for survival or escape.

Our bodies do their best based on the information we have and the things we've learned in life, but they haven't yet evolved to distinguish perfectly between stress types—especially emotional stress caused by modern issues. Being in the vicinity of a hungry lion and having stage fright can sometimes provoke the same kind of physiological fight-or-flight response, even when stage fright might be better suited for a tend-and-befriend response. If we *were* confronting a lion attack, we would find our ability to run faster to be quite useful. However, when we're experiencing our most common everyday stressors, the physical side effects—increased breathing rate, speeding heartbeat, and tensing muscles—become unfortunate distractions or roadblocks. Mentally, we might not be well-served by becoming angry and aggressive whenever something goes wrong in our lives, or constantly avoiding our problems. Furthermore, having a difficult childhood and adolescence or role models with ineffective stress habits can train us for unhealthy patterns.

It is especially important to know that length of time matters when under stress. Our physical stressors (like escaping violence) tend to not be one-time events, especially in cases of bullying and dangerous households. We encounter our stressors regularly in continual cycles or even on a daily basis—studying and taking tests, performing in extracurriculars or playing sports, getting into college, meeting deadlines, managing expectations for school and careers, encountering discrimination, living in poverty, living in dangerous neighborhoods, or surviving unsupportive, neglectful, or abusive households. The lived daily fear of an unsafe home or a toxic environment can be ongoing. The long-term emotional fallout of a bad breakup, online harassment, or poor grades might stretch over days or weeks. College applications are a months-long process.

Sometimes we hear the criticism that humans aren't as "tough" as they used to be, which is an impossible and meaningless comparison. Most modern stressors aren't about seeking food or navigating a physical landscape and its challenges, but this doesn't mean they aren't life-or-death—they're just about surviving the world *differently* than we did hundreds or thousands of years ago. For example, failing out of school becomes a life-or-death concern when we consider that not being able to get a job can mean a lifetime of struggling to feed ourselves. The nature of our problems has changed, but they aren't less important or serious.

And if we're constantly feeling stressed? Soon we will be mentally and physically burned out and sick. Chronic stress outlasts a single demanding moment. If our bodies don't receive the signal that we are in a safe state, we can't rest and recharge. We can't relax. Instead, we remain in a constant state of heightened, disruptive stress—as if we have to be ready to outrun a lion at all times. That is far from healthy.

When our bodies continually delay long-term processes in favor of getting through the short-term moment, our natural systems are thrown out of order. Essential tasks our organs need to complete don't get done properly. The end result of this constant strain is disease and disorder. In fact, some estimates place up to *75 percent* of all medical issues as originating from chronic stress.[19]

For example, having our normal digestion disrupted on occasion is unremarkable. Having our normal digestion disrupted constantly can lead to serious sickness and even long-term disease. Think of all the ways digestion can go wrong: stomach ulcers, vomiting, diarrhea, constipation, and metabolic disorders, including getting inadequate nutrition from the food we eat or our bodies storing nutrients and fat in unhealthy ways. Remember that the stress hormone cortisol—which tells the body to hoard its nutrients and stockpile fat reserves in case of food shortage—can have long-term impacts on blood sugar, leading to metabolic issues, growth disruption, diabetes, and obesity.

Since stress can increase the heart rate to pump additional nutrients through our bloodstream, it raises our blood pressure. As a chronic issue, this puts strain on the heart over time and can lead to high blood pressure and heart conditions. The stress response temporarily suppresses our immune system in favor of fueling other systems. This isn't a serious concern for brief windows of time, but having a consistently weakened immune system leaves us vulnerable to infections and unable to fight disease adequately. In each of the body's systems, the difference between short-term and long-term stress responses is the difference between health and disorder. This is why chronic stress can lead to all kinds of serious mental and physical conditions.

Our bodies have many powerful survival mechanisms enabled by stress, but chronic stress locks us in a state of crisis—our thoughts can spiral repetitively, our sleep patterns become interrupted or irregular, and our immune systems grow weak. When experiencing chronic stress, it may feel like we're constantly reacting to problems emotionally and physically. It's normal to have emotions like fear, anger, and sadness (and to feel these things very strongly) during stressful times. However, feeling locked in these emotional states, along with other stress symptoms that disrupt our everyday functioning, ability to form healthy relationships, and overall well-being, suggests our stress has become chronic. Signs of unmanageable, chronic stress include:

- Ongoing difficulty with managing emotions, including feelings of anger, fear, depression, anxiety, or even numbness

- Increased or decreased appetite

- Difficulty focusing/concentrating

- Disrupted sleep patterns, insomnia, and nightmares

- Physical illness, including headaches and stomachaches

- Reliance on or increased use of alcohol, drugs, and other substances[20]

Experiencing chronic stress doesn't mean that our stress is caused by more "serious" issues than normal, although it can be. It means the duration of our stress (and the physiological, neurological, and psychological impact of our stress responses) has extended longer than is effective for daily functioning.

Think about it this way: stress is a short-term solution that interrupts our daily functioning. But even solutions can become problems if daily functioning doesn't resume! Surviving a difficult situation, like finding a temporary shelter to hide from a lion attack, is the first step.

Stress sets us up to achieve safety so that we can get back to our lives growing, learning, and experiencing new things. Stress isn't the long-term solution, which is surviving long enough to build a shelter where no lions can get in so that we can rest. If we can't find a long-term solution to resolve the situation that triggered the stress—we never find a shelter, never stop running, and never get back to living our lives—eventually our bodies will become exhausted and in worse shape than when we encountered the stressor.

If we feel constantly drained or burned out by stress, we might be experiencing chronic stress. There are many ways to improve our relationship with stress, however. And even if our stress isn't chronic, learning more about how stress works and building coping strategies will help maintain those healthy stress levels and keep stress from becoming chronic.

How has the pandemic affected your stress in the long-term?

Lizzie

I live with my dad and stepmom, and I have three much younger half-siblings. There's a lot of noise when there's three kids under the age of four in the house, and I try to be understanding about that. I don't live with my mom because she's always in and out of these little apartments and has a hard time keeping a job. It's either moving every two months with someone I don't really trust or having a stable home with a lot of noise. I know which one I prefer, and it's the noise.

But basically, that means I'm the daycare and a student at the same time. It's been months like this. I'm literally on my laptop in a class with everything on mute because I don't want everyone to see that I'm holding a crying baby. Which, I guess now that I think about it would probably start a funny rumor that I have a secret baby. Or I'm in the kitchen missing something because I'm fixing snacks. I love my brothers and sister, but I'm tired.

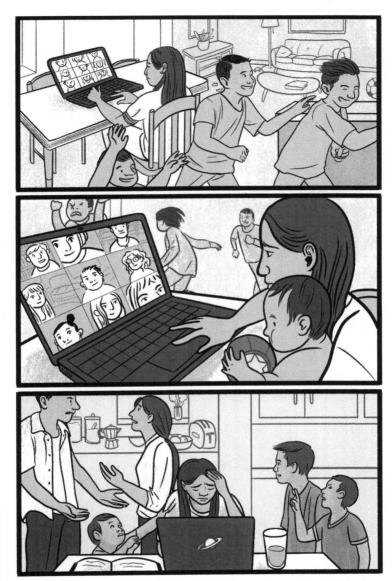

Lizzie's large family makes remote learning due to the pandemic difficult, as her parents expect her to help out with her younger siblings while in class. *Illustration by Kate Haberer.*

Everyone else is working in their bedroom. Or, like, by the pool. Meanwhile, I'm in the middle of chaos. Daycare is expensive. I'm old enough to watch them. But people were laughing about how easy remote classes were because you barely had to do anything and you show up in your pajamas, and that was just not my experience. I miss proper school. I'd do anything to go back there, my calm place.

Anna

Maybe it's because the refrigerator is right there, and I'm home a lot more, but I've been stress eating so much. I have always really fought with my weight and struggled with my body image. Knowing I'm eating too much just sends me on a cycle of more stress eating. I've probably gained fifteen pounds.

I say "probably." I'm trying to downplay it, but I *know* I gained about fifteen pounds. My school uniform shirts don't quite button properly now, so I had to get new ones.

Have you ever experienced a stressor that didn't go away? What sort of things cause you long-term stress?

Mattie

I just don't fit in very well with my family. Not belonging kind of . . . doesn't go away. My four older siblings are all very much the golden children who are really talented in various ways. Almost all of them are athletic or artistic or smart. I'm a bit of a mess as far as my family is concerned. I think they don't mean to make me the outcast, but it just happens. My brothers and sisters don't bully me, exactly, but sometimes it's like there's always not quite enough room in the family for me. I'm the youngest and was kind of an unexpected surprise. Basically, I think my siblings had more time growing up together, so they have their own little club. I'm not in it. They have their jokes and memories of stuff that I wasn't around for and stuff like that.

It can be really stressful because it's like our family is a game of musical chairs, and I'm always the one out when we're short a chair. My older sister hated sharing her room with me because until I was born, everyone had their own rooms. Once I wasn't in a high chair, there wasn't enough room at the table for all of us to sit in normal chairs, so I usually sit at our kitchen bar area instead of at the table to eat. They never wanted me around hanging out with their friends because I was the annoying baby sister, so mostly I just spent a lot of time playing games online or whatever.

One of my friends was saying that the movie *Home Alone* was stupid since it's based on this ridiculous premise that parents could actually forget one of their kids at home. I told him that I could see how that could happen. It wouldn't surprise me in the least if my family accidentally forgot me when they went on a trip.

A lot of these things are really minor, like my Christmas stocking doesn't match everyone else's because mine got bought separately. I know that my brothers and sisters wouldn't see why that matters, or they'd make a joke about me being an accident if I pointed it out. Mostly, they just take it for granted that they belong together. That bothers me too. They don't realize how *nice* it is to belong.

Leila

My acne is at the front of my mind all the time. It's my face, so it's not like I can ignore it all the time. Sometimes I'll forget, then I walk past a mirror or go to the bathroom and there it is again. I can't put on makeup to cover it because that only makes it worse. I have a dark complexion, so the scars are even darker.

My family thinks that my acne is hilarious in this very weird way—like my dad or aunts and uncles will always joke about how it's a sign that I'm a *real* teenager. Every family gathering. Oh, you've grown up so much, look at you looking like a real teenager with the pimples and everything. Who says that? I don't know how that's funny when it clearly bothers me. Or if I ask them to stop joking about it, they'll pile on more about how I have acne *and* I'm sensitive about it, so I'm *really* a teenager now.

Maddilyn

I know this is going to sound weird, but my art, which is my whole world, is always a stressor. It's the thing that I do to feel better, to take things that bother me and make them beautiful. But I'm a perfectionist, so what I'm picturing never comes out. Even if everyone says what I painted is pretty good or really good, I know that wasn't what I meant to do.

Maybe it's not the art itself but the perfectionism that's the problem, I guess. I just don't know how to make something and be satisfied with it.

Oh, and that all fits in with the stress from college applications. Wow. They're the worst. I'm freaking out about picking the right college for me. My family couldn't afford to do any real college tours or college visits, and even if we could, there's the pandemic.

I want to go to an art school, but my parents don't think I can have a good job with an art degree. And some of the best art schools are super expensive if you don't get a great scholarship. I want to double major in painting and filmmaking, so I've been working like crazy trying to put together a scholarship portfolio. I've spent at least a year making things for it.

Lindsey

Everything about social media. Would I want to live in any other time period? No. I'm not saying I want to live without my phone or anything.

But I'm not going to lie, I'll scroll through my feeds for hours and get nothing done. I never feel better about myself afterward. It doesn't matter how much you tell yourself that it's all fake, no one is that beautiful or that happy or perfect all the time. It still looks better than my boring life and my regular face.

I refuse to check my screen time, by the way. I don't even want to know how much of my life I'm wasting. It would probably just make me more stressed if I did know how many hours a day I've burned.

Cam

In middle school, there was a guy named Stephen who picked on me every day. Every single day. I had to ride the bus with him, so there wasn't even a way to avoid him.

At the time I was still presenting as female, although I'm out as nonbinary now. I went through a time where I tried really hard to be more traditionally "girly." Stephen would find something to say about my hair being short, or my watch being for boys, or whatever it was that he noticed that day. If I wore makeup, he'd announce it to everyone really loudly. Or if I got my hair cut shorter, or whatever. If I looked more girly, it wasn't good enough, and if I looked less girly, he'd say I was disgusting.

There wasn't anything he couldn't make into a joke about me secretly being a boy. While I know now that I don't want to necessarily be a boy, I was still trying really hard to pretend I did want to be a girl.

I couldn't walk out the door without going over everything I was wearing or carrying to make sure it wasn't too tomboyish. And my family didn't even give me a hard time about what I wanted to wear. My other nonbinary friends struggled with that, but for me it was Stephen. If I wanted shorts from the guys' section and a shirt from the girls' section, my mom never said anything at all. I'm sure if I saw him now, he'd have something to say about me being nonbinary, too.

I think some people just can't help but be unsupportive of others. Whatever it is about them or their lives that they're unhappy with, they have to make sure everyone else feels unhappy too. Stephen got under my skin like that for three years! What a nightmare.

Tegan

My mom has cancer. There isn't a minute that goes by that I don't think about that. If I'm not careful with COVID-19 exposure, it could kill her. She's doing okay but she's in active treatment. She has basically no immune system. Before the vaccine was developed, we were so scared.

Most of the family is vaccinated now, so my friends think I should stop worrying. But it's still always a worry. My little sister and brother are too young to get vaccinated right now, though we're hoping they'll change the age restrictions soon. My mom can't get the vaccine at all until she's done with her treatment.

Basically, I'm always checking with myself. Did I wash my hands? Did I wash them for long enough or did I rush it? Did I keep my distance from people? My state has a mask law, but every now and then they lift it, and that makes me nervous too. I don't care if people think I'm paranoid or being too careful.

I didn't see any of my friends in person for months when the pandemic first started. Any of them, not even one. Just FaceTime and Zoom calls for months. A couple of them kind of suggested I was being dramatic. Like, "I think you're making a big deal over your mom, but it's not really that big of a deal. She'll be fine."

It's really hard for me to forgive them for not taking it seriously. I get that they don't live with someone who's incredibly sick and could die, but it's something I *have* to worry about.

HOW DOES STRESS IMPACT ADOLESCENTS DIFFERENTLY?

Stress, especially long-term stress, can be even more concerning for adolescents than adults for a multitude of reasons. One is quite simply because both life changes and the unknown itself are stressors. Adolescence is a series of transitions, milestones, and big choices across a wide social, psychological, and physiological spectrum. By extension, experiencing youth means experiencing inherently stressful challenges as our bodies and minds develop into adulthood.

Our confidence in decision-making might not be as strong in youth. Relying on prior experiences can help us predict what their next right step will be (or at least feel more confident in making our choices). Adults might stress less about their choices even if they're making an ineffective or unhealthy choice simply because of confidence gained from age and experience. Alternatively, adolescence means facing more unknown leaps with less history to guide our choices or predict an outcome. It doesn't mean we're less likely to make an effective choice, but it does mean we might lack confidence and experience increased stress as a result.

Another reason is the nature of the maturing adolescent brain. Major neurological and hormonal changes during adolescence impact brain development, increasing teenage vulnerability to depression and anxiety. This is one underlying reason why mood disorders like depression nearly double from 8.4 percent of thirteen-year-olds to 15.4 percent of eighteen-year-olds.[21]

Studies have shown that some brain areas are particularly sensitive to stress, including the hippocampus, prefrontal cortex, and amygdala. These are the same areas under development during adolescence. This means that stress can impact our learning, decision-making abilities, and attention spans, all while affecting how strongly we respond to stress. Furthermore, stress responses occur more quickly in adolescence than adulthood because the prefrontal cortex, which manages emotions, controls impulses, assesses danger, and can call off the stress response, is the last part of the brain to fully develop.[22]

Since the brain uses hormonal signals to activate the stress response in the rest of the body, it is unsurprising that adolescents—already experiencing a phase of major hormonal shifts—experience "heightened stress-induced hormonal responses."[23] During times of stress, the adolescent body releases more stress hormones that affect teens for longer time periods. Most importantly, the adult brain recovers to normal, post-stress functioning after about ten days, whereas the adolescent brain—still under structural development—seems to retain some of these stress-induced changes over the long term.[24]

Therefore, the neurological effects might vary between adults and adolescents experiencing the same stressful event. Many adolescents have experienced adults undermining our experiences, suggesting we are being dramatic or are exaggerating. These demeaning suggestions fail to take brain chemistry into account. What we feel is different—literally—depending on our age and brain chemistry.

Furthermore, chronic stress becomes problematic in adolescence because long-term exposure to stress hormones like cortisol can impact our bodies' growth and development. We know that there is a direct correlation between serious adverse childhood experiences (ACEs) and abnormal bodily changes and/or developing health challenges later in adulthood.[25] While these ACEs are traumatic, including emotional, physical, and sexual abuse, neglect, and serious family upheaval, they reveal the strain of chronic stress on developing child and adolescent bodies.

One of the most important takeaways here is that how we experience and cope with stress in adolescence can affect how our brain learns to process stress and can set up long-term habits for our future. During childhood and adolescence, our brains are growing and maturing into the brains we'll carry with us for a lifetime. Yes, the downside is that this growth makes the young brain sensitive to challenges and outside input that stimulate it (all those stressors!). The positive news about adolescent sensitivity to stress also means that this is the prime time to build healthy habits into our brain structures to make those habits easy to access for life. (This applies to any habit learned in youth, whether healthy or not; our impulses become easier or harder depending on whether we're working with or against what we've learned from a young age.)

Already struggled with some ineffective coping or learned some difficult habits to break? Don't worry! Adolescence is *not* our only opportunity for the brain to hardwire in effective ways of handling and responding to stress. Though our brain is most capable of building neural pathways (which guide our impulses to communicate with the rest of the body) during adolescence, it is a myth that the brain cannot learn, grow, change, and make new pathways past a certain age. We now know that the brain never stops learning and changing in response to new information; it simply gets a little harder in adulthood.

Now is a great time to learn, improve, and grow coping skills, but there will be opportunities in the future as well.

What helps you unwind when you're experiencing long-term stress? What helps you let even the most stubborn stressors go?

Charlie

Music. If there's anything that can make it all go away for a little while, it's the right song turned up loud. I'll play it ten times in a row sometimes.

Jamie

I'm a big fan of puzzles and logic games. I'll keep a tab open on my browser for a jigsaw puzzle website and a sudoku website. When I'm matching shapes or counting up numbers, everything else fades away. I'll do it on my phone or on my laptop between things, whenever I need to take a minute and chill out.

Lately, I've been doing these grid image puzzles called nonograms that my teacher showed me. She saw me doing a jigsaw online after a test and showed me the nonograms website she uses. It was pretty cool that she understood that I needed to relax and wasn't mad. Anyway, nonograms come in either color or black-and-white designs, and you have to figure out whether to put a solid tile or a blank tile in each square. It makes a picture when you're done. I find it literally impossible to feel anything but relaxed when I'm just counting out tiles and clicking squares to fill them with color.

Maddilyn

Reading is my escape. The best books are like, I forget that I'm reading, I'm actually living inside the story. Some people are like that with movies, but I like how with books I can fill in the visual blanks in my mind.

ACTIVITY BREAK: MYSTERIES AND WONDER

Neil Armstrong, the first person to walk on the moon, said, "Mystery creates wonder and wonder is the basis of man's desire to understand." A curious human mind seeks answers to the mysteries just beyond our understanding, and remaining open to wonder can help us stay invested and intrigued with the world and life, even on our darkest days.

Take ten minutes to think about mysteries you would like to solve. These can be lighthearted mysteries (*why* are so many of my socks missing their mate?) or more complex ones (such as the origins and meaning of the Voynich manuscript, a book from around the 1400s handwritten in an unknown language that remains untranslated to this day). If you can't think of any mysteries off the top of your head, a quick internet search (try "interesting mysteries" or "unanswered questions") can turn up all kinds of mysteries to ponder.

What kind of things do you wonder about? What questions would you like answered? What sort of things fascinate you that you'd like to learn more about? Try to avoid mysteries that make you feel dread or anxiety; consider mysteries that make you feel curious or filled with wonder instead.

CHAPTER THREE

EXPLORING ANXIETY

WHEN FEAR BECOMES DISORDER

In its ideal functioning state, stress comes from an appropriate trigger (that is, an internal or external pressure) and is resolved quickly. In the previous chapter, we talked about how stress becomes unhealthy when it continues on longer than a brief moment of survival. Another form of disordered stress is an extreme state of stress that is stronger than the stressor calls for, or occurs without a stressor at all. When there are no actual pressures but our bodies carry all the symptoms of stress, the *fear* of a stressor that hasn't happened yet produces anxiety.

Like stress, fear has its place in every healthy human's life. Fear's inhibition system keeps us from making dangerous choices, like approaching snarling animals or jumping from dangerous heights. However, when fear affects our daily functioning, makes us try to control every little aspect of our lives, or keeps us in a state of avoidance, it becomes a problem.

Like stress, there are healthy and unhealthy versions of anxiety. We all have a loose sense of what anxiety is—we describe it as a general feeling of concern or worrying. Anxiety can be a healthy and appropriate response to life's difficulties and stressful encounters. If we didn't experience anxiety in response to an upsetting event, that might be *more* concerning than when we do. In these circumstances, there's an identifiable cause, experience, or event provoking the anxiety.

The medical definition of anxiety as a disorder, however, is when it occurs in a way that is "either out of proportion to the threat or with no discernible cause."[1] The numbers show that adolescents suffering from anxiety are not alone. In fact, anxiety disorders are the most common disorders affecting children and adolescents; these include generalized anxiety disorder (GAD), social anxiety, phobias, and panic attacks, among others. We know that prior to the pandemic, about 30 percent of adolescents reported experiencing anxiety prior to turning eighteen; we also know that 80 percent of them will never receive treatment of any kind, and only 1 percent will get treatment in the same year their anxiety begins.[2]

Doctors and therapists use guidelines covering a range of signs and symptoms to distinguish appropriate anxiety as a stress response from anxiety as a disorder. Beyond having excessive stress and worry, the specific list of anxiety's warning signs will vary slightly depending on which guidelines a country follows, but these guidelines are nearly identical. In the United States, a manual called *The Diagnostic and Statistical Manual of Mental Disorders* (often referred to as the DSM) published by the American Psychiatric Association determines the diagnostic criteria for anxiety. In the United Kingdom and many other countries, the World Health Organization's *International Classification of Diseases* sets the criteria. There is no exact checklist because like all diseases and disorders, anxiety varies for every individual; we will not fit every sign and symptom perfectly.

The equation for a mental health diagnosis combines a series of factors: our feelings and behaviors, the duration for which we've experienced them, and the unhealthy impact these feelings and behaviors have had on our daily functioning. For generalized anxiety disorder, one of the most common anxiety disorders, the primary signs doctors and therapists look for in addition to persistent worry lasting for several months include:

- Concern about the future and potential misfortunes, nervousness, and/or irritability

- Difficulty with concentration and focus

- Restlessness, fidgeting, tense muscles, and inability to relax

- Disrupted sleeping

- Tension headaches, dizziness, rapid heartbeat, rapid breathing, stomachaches, and dry mouth[3]

We don't need to experience every single one of these signs—and these aren't necessarily the *only* signs of anxiety—but to provide an accurate diagnosis, our specialist will be looking for some combination of these affecting our lives.

If our anxiety emerges as more severe than the stressor that prompted it or we are often anxious without a clear cause, we might be experiencing anxiety as a disorder. Even if our experiences don't meet these criteria for a disorder, learning more and developing coping strategies give us a good foundation for avoiding anxiety problems later in life.

In many cases, GAD emerges as looping thought patterns asking worst-case scenario "what if?" questions about whatever we value in our lives: *What if I fail my final exams? What if my significant other breaks up with me? What if I fall during dance tryouts? What if my parents get divorced?* Some of these concerns may seem reasonable in light of their importance to our lives, and yet if they become a disruption to our ability to reasonably understand that most of these things *won't* happen—or that if they do, it will be unfortunate but we will survive—then they are a problem keeping us from enjoying life.

Common to GAD are two ineffective coping strategies: the impulse to over-plan or control situations, and/or avoiding situations altogether. Ultimately, we can experience a lot of frustration trying to control all the uncontrollable details of our lives so that we don't experience what we worry about. And when we shut down the possibility of an experience because something might go wrong, we miss out on life completely.

Another common anxiety disorder is panic attacks. Panic attacks are rapid, intense moments in which we are seized with fear, and they can be extremely frightening experiences. The signs and symptoms of

DATE April 21

ANXIETY IN REVIEW

TODAY'S CONCERNS — Really struggling with Mr. G's class. Can't follow the lecture. I'm exhausted, but haven't been sleeping well.

SMALL STEPS UNDER MY CONTROL

Ask for lecture notes from someone in Mr. G's class. Talk to him after school for extra help.

Try to put my phone away an hour before bedtime & take a hot shower first to get me relaxed for bed.

HOW I RESPONDED THIS TIME

Got nervous about talking to Mr. G, so I just got lecture notes from Bree. Forgot about putting phone away, but I did take the hot shower & I feel ready for bed.

NEXT TIME I WOULD LIKE TO...

Really going to talk to Mr. G tomorrow. Bree said he helped her last week and it was fine.

Anxiety can make us believe our problems are too large to manage, but if we can approach our issues with small steps, we make it manageable. There are many things out of our control, but it's useful to look at our concerns, map out what we can do about them—even in little ways—and make a plan for next time. Download a free blank version of this review sheet from the author's website at christiecognevich.com. *Illustration by Christie Cognevich.*

panic attacks include a moment of extreme fear or worry combined with the sudden onset of:

- Irregular or rapid heartbeat

- Sweating or chills

- Shortness of breath, rapid breathing, choking, chest pain

- Nausea

- Dizziness, lightheadedness

- Fear of insanity or death[4]

Panic attacks can be such a disturbing physical experience that they may feel like a heart attack or like we're dying.

While panic attacks can begin occurring anytime in life as a disordered response to stressors, they're often provoked by major life events such as leaving home for college, getting married, or losing a family member.[5] Because adolescence is, as we noted before, a time of many "firsts" and life changes, it is unsurprising that about a third of adolescents will experience panic attacks in a given year.[6]

What was your first experience recognizing that your stress and/or anxiety were severe or out of control?

Abby

When I started lying to cover up my anxiety, I knew I had a problem. My parents are really brilliant, successful people. My dad works as an engineer, and my mom is a data analyst, so they're very STEM-oriented and really, for anything academic they have the highest expectations.

I'm afraid of letting them down. I think if I don't get a full-ride scholarship to a top college, they'll cry. I'm not dumb, I work hard, and I'm pretty decent. But I'm not perfect, and they have a lot of

Since Abby's parents put so much pressure on her to maintain straight As, she started making fake progress reports to show her grades being better than they were. *Illustration by Kate Haberer.*

expectations and pressure for perfect. If I don't get straight As, it's not even like they give just me a hard time—they give my teachers a hard time, too. That's really embarrassing.

When our progress reports got mailed home last year, I knew I had a B+ on there. I worked hard, had a rough time, and it just was what it was. And yeah, it's just a progress report, so there's time to improve the grade before the report card. Tell that to my parents. I knew they'd be upset. I couldn't live with their disappointment and their standards when I was working so hard and going to a tutor during my independent study period.

I took the real progress report out of the mailbox, scanned it, edited the file to change the B+ to an A- and then printed a new copy.

I left the report on the kitchen table and just felt so resentful that this is what I ended up doing. I ended up getting an A- on the report card in the end, so I told myself I don't have to feel guilty. But I don't feel like I should have had to be dishonest, either. That's when I knew something had to give between their perfect standards and my mental health.

Lately I've been kind of mentioning to them that I'm feeling pretty overwhelmed and sort of feeling out their response. I don't know. It's been okay—they haven't been *unsupportive*—but I'm not ready to have the full conversation with them about what their pressure is doing to me.

Alivia

There's a sort of funny story behind how I started to understand how much constant tension I was under and that I might have a serious anxiety problem. So, I know exactly what it stress feels like in my body—it feels like an organ, like I've got this knot like right here, right under where my breastbone is. It's just always been there.

But when I was maybe seventeen or eighteen, I felt myself relax for the first time in years. I mean that literally. For the first time in literally years and years, I was surrounded by people I liked, and I was pretty sure that I knew they liked me. I was sprawled out on the floor and we were watching one of the movie versions of *Pride and Prejudice*. And I felt good. Then something just sort of . . . dissolved in my chest. This sort of looseness took over my body.

And here's the kind-of-funny part: in response to that, I had a panic attack so bad that I went to the hospital because it felt like some structural part of me had just . . . disintegrated. Like, I thought I'd snapped a muscle or broken a bone somehow. I thought there had to be a health problem, that there was something wrong.

I just thought, oh, my God, something has gone horribly wrong inside my body. I don't know what it is, but something, just something that's supposed to be there *isn't*, it's gone. And I panicked. Nothing wrong. It turns out that I didn't know how badly I'd been suffering for years to the point that feeling good sent me to the hospital.

So that's how I know what I feel when my anxiety is out of control now—I get that hard knot right in my chest that I carry around feeling constantly tense and constantly tight around my lungs a little.

Bella

When my parents were divorcing, they'd have these screaming fights. My mom would just be standing there with tears pouring down her cheeks while she shouted and my dad would be standing there cold and unfeeling while he said horrible things right back, just without raising his voice. And I'd watch them doing this every single night and feel like someone was stabbing an ice pick into my chest. Right near the top of my lungs, I guess, right in the center here.

I would have done anything to get them to just stop doing that. It went away for a little while when they finally separated.

A couple years later, when I was thirteen or fourteen, I'd start getting that sharp pain in my chest again whenever I got worried about something. If I thought I was going to get in trouble for something? Stab, right in the chest. Worried about my grades? Stab again.

The first time my mom introduced a new guy she was dating named Dan, the guy who eventually became my stepdad, I had the worst panic attack I'd ever had before. It started with the stabbing pain, but then I started shaking and crying. I couldn't breathe. There were just tears and snot pouring down my face while I was making these choking noises. And when I think about it, I think I was hearing these noises I was making and that was making the panic attack worse. Like I couldn't breathe and I thought I was choking, so I was choking harder because of it.

I really freaked Dan out, but he's a decent guy. He stuck around, and the good news is that he was the one who told my mom that it looked like I was having panic attacks and she should check in about that.

My mom took me to the doctor. Now I have a prescription to take whenever I have panic attacks or I think I'm going to have one. It's actually an allergy medication, like Benadryl. It makes you sleepy, so it calms you down. I don't think it's a super-strong prescription, but it works for me.

ACTIVITY BREAK: TAKING SPACE, TELLING STORIES

One common struggle with generalized anxiety disorder is how overpowering and "sticky" a thought can become when we worry about it incessantly. An effective habit when thoughts get stuck is to step back from ourselves/our minds by naming or labeling the recurring thought like the title of a book, television show, or movie. Social worker Rachel Willimott offers the following example: "if your mind regularly worries about appearing awkward to others, you might name the thought *The I Am So Awkward Story*."[7]

Take a few minutes to think about some recurring fears or worries you have, that loud inner critic we often suffer from, and give them some names. Do you have a thought named *The I Am So Awkward Story*? What about the *I Talk Too Loudly Story* like the one I tell myself sometimes? The idea behind this activity is that by naming our anxious thoughts and the lies they tell us, we take some space from them and see them for what they are: simply stories we tell ourselves, not real parts of us.

CHAPTER FOUR

FIRST STEPS TO FINDING SUPPORT

REACHING OUT

We've been talking about how stress goes wrong using this book's guiding belief that understanding what our bodies are doing and why can provide some measure of relief. Making stress less mysterious, making the sensations we feel emotionally and physically make sense, is one way of coping.

When we are in serious distress and at a crisis point, simply having that knowledge may seem overwhelming. The clarity it provides might seem too little, too late.

If stress has become unmanageable or chronic, or has developed into an anxiety disorder, the first step is to reach out to a trusted adult.

This can be any adult figure with whom we feel comfortable sharing personal details, including family members, friends, teachers, coaches, counselors, or religious leaders. If we have unsupportive family or a troubled family structure, this trusted adult can help us come up with strategies to work with those difficult family situations.

Consider also what would help us feel more comfortable when reaching out. Would we rather be with a friend, or would we rather talk alone? Where and when would it be easiest to open up? Which is better for us: email, text, phone call, online, in person? We have lots of options that might lower our anxiety if we struggle with calls or face-to-face interactions.

Harder still is when we don't think we have any supportive adults that we feel comfortable with—or we don't feel comfortable reaching out to someone we know in person *yet*. However, many resources for nonjudgmental, helpful people are available online or via text and phone; they can support us in finding someone we *can* talk to in person. Communication helps build support systems. Keep talking. Keep reaching out.

Though stress can lead to anxiety, depression, and poor health in general, talking to someone can make a world of difference in lessening shame, making connections, and feeling better.

MENTAL HEALTH HOTLINES AND RESOURCES

Remember, when facing a mental health emergency, including thinking about suicide or self-harm, call one of the help lines listed below or go to the emergency room immediately.

Even if we feel unable to act or don't know what to do to help our stress, others can help. Pause, breathe, then reach out to one of the resources listed here as soon as possible. Many safe, confidential, free, immediate options are available for us to talk, text, or chat online with someone if we are in crisis.

These services are designed to provide people who can talk to and stay with us until we have moved out of extreme distress into a calmer mindset. We never have to experience crisis alone.

We do not need to hesitate or ask ourselves if our issues are serious enough to call any of these numbers. These options are available for *anyone* who needs to talk about *any* issue, regardless of the "seriousness" of our problems or mental health condition.

United States:

- Call 911 for an emergency, or call the 24/7 National Suicide Prevention Hotline at 1-800-273-8255. There are options for Spanish speakers and the deaf/hard of hearing.

- If more comfortable texting, the Crisis Text Line (https://www.cri sistextline.org/) is a free text message service available for people in crisis, available 24/7 in English or Spanish. Text HOME to 741741. It is available on WhatsApp and Facebook Messenger as well.

- The National Alliance on Mental Illness (NAMI) HelpLine (nami .org) can be reached Monday through Friday, 10 a.m. to 10 p.m. EST at 1-800-950-NAMI or via email at info@nami.org.

- If more comfortable texting, NAMI has a free text message service for people in crisis, available 24/7. Text NAMI to 741741.

- NAMI also has an online chat feature available on their website.

Canada:

- Call 911 for an emergency, or the 24/7 Kids Help phone service (anyone under the age of twenty) at 1-800-668-6868, or Crisis Services Canada (no age restriction) at 1-833-456-4566. Quebec residents can call Crisis Services at 1-866-277-3553.

- If more comfortable texting, the Crisis Text Line (https://www .crisistextline.ca/) is a free text message service for people in crisis, available 24/7 in English or French. Text HOME (in English) or PARLER (in French) to 686868.

United Kingdom:

- Call 999 for an emergency, or the National Health Service's First Response Service for mental health at 111, Option 2.

- If more comfortable texting, Shout (https://giveusashout.org/) is a free text message service for people in crisis, available 24/7. Text SHOUT to 85258.

Ireland:

- Call 112 for an emergency, or the Samaritans emotional support helpline at 116 123.

- If more comfortable texting, the Crisis Text Line (https://text50808 .ie/) is a free text message service for people in crisis, available 24/7. Text HELLO to 50808.

Australia:

- Call 000 for an emergency, or the 24/7 Kids Helpline phone service (anyone under the age of twenty-five) at 1800 55 1800, or Lifeline (no age restriction) at 13 11 14.

- Both Lifeline (https://www.lifeline.org.au/) and Kids Helpline (https://www.kidshelpline.com.au/) have online chat features available on their respective websites.

- If more comfortable texting, the Lifeline Text is available from 12 p.m. to 6 a.m. AEDT at 0477 13 11 14.

Furthermore, mental health resources are available to us regardless of our identity, circumstances, or economic situation. In the United States (211.org) and Canada (211.ca), 211 is a free and confidential resource to help people of all ages find free or low-cost mental health support and services, including help getting food or healthcare. Call 211 to talk, to find support for mental health, if hungry, or if needing help getting out of a dangerous or abusive household or relationship.

Many free support groups are designed to help individuals with a variety of issues, interests, and identities. Check chapter 14, "Quick Guide to Resources" in this book as a starting point. Another useful starting point is the National Alliance on Mental Illness (nami.org). Remember that local libraries, universities, and places of worship also offer many community resources, support groups, and sometimes even assistance finding funds to get the help needed. We may find that we feel most comfortable in a support group that isn't necessarily mental health–focused, but instead gives us a community based on our interests and hobbies, a group where we feel safe to build a support system around ourselves.

We do not have to be in an immediate state of crisis to contact any of the mental health hotlines listed above. If we feel like we need to talk to someone, no matter how big or small the issue, we can reach out.

Even if our stress doesn't reach the level of disorder—and remember, some stress is a healthy state if it doesn't affect our daily functioning or become chronic—the resources available at these mental health organization websites can be highly informative and useful in continuing to maintain our well-being.

What kinds of communities and resources have you found to help you with your stress?

Jamie

I'm sure many people have a similar story, but I found a lot of support from the "nerd" community. I have a condition that affects my fine motor skills, so I have a few little twitches, some trembling, and sometimes my hands are too weak to grip things. Most days it doesn't bother me, but when I get stressed out, it becomes much more noticeable.

In middle school, I was really self-conscious about limping sometimes and having to sit out of PE class. I spent my PE class period in the library, and spent a lot of time just getting into reading fantasy books. When I found out about tabletop roleplaying games, it just seemed like a natural extension of the books I was into. At first, I was nervous and self-conscious because if you've ever played tabletop games you know there's a lot of dice rolling, which, you know, I have shaky hands.

But it's never been an issue at all. I think honestly if anyone said anything about it, my gaming friends would kick them out of the game. Everyone comes to the game to step into a character's shoes, so we're all leaving a little something from the real world behind when we play. I spend most of the night laughing and having a great time. There's never a moment where I'm thinking about how I dropped the dice or whatever.

During the pandemic, we just shifted our gaming sessions to Zoom. It works fine, and one of the cool things is that we always went over to one person's house and have never seen anyone else's spaces. Getting to see people in their own environment is sort of neat. Thinking of it in that way took the disappointment out of not getting together with everyone in person.

Mattie

Since I don't fit in very well with my family, I spent a lot of time online growing up. I'm a lot younger, so when my mom was driving my siblings to sports practice or we were at everyone's games, I'd be on my iPad to keep me occupied. Maybe more than was healthy, but it worked out okay because I found out that I really like coding.

It began with a website called Scratch that lets you move blocks of code around. It's really easy—I started when I was maybe seven or eight, so it's not too complicated to pick up. And actually, for anyone who's considering starting coding, I really recommend it. It's supposed to be for kids and teenagers, but anyone can use it.

From there, I decided I wanted to code real working games, which was way more ambitious than I realized as a kid. At least, the games I wanted to make weren't realistic for me at the time! I started talking to people on forums as I tried to get better and learn more. I'm sure I was mostly talking to people who were a *lot* older than me, but everyone was pretty helpful. I think for the most part if you go somewhere and are genuinely interested in learning and are asking questions, people will try to be helpful.

My mom saw that I was into coding and didn't really understand it herself, but it kept me busy and happy. She asked my grandparents to chip in to pay for some coding classes at this place nearby. They have a colored belt system that's kind of like karate, so you can move your way up as you learn more complicated code starting with JavaScript and then moving up.

Recently a guy I was talking to said it was cool to meet someone who had a real passion for something, and I guess that's a good word to describe it. Coding was an escape, but it became a passion.

Now I spend a lot of time on forums helping people just getting started, answering questions. It's kind of like I'm helping my younger self, which is a good feeling. I like being part of a helpful community that once helped me a lot.

Tegan

I consider my therapist a huge part of my support resources. My parents sent me to a therapist when my mom was first diagnosed with cancer as a way of helping me cope. I didn't want to go at first, but I'm glad they made me. I was a few years younger than I am now, and I don't think I understood at first how hard it was going to be for me to see my mom come home from treatments and get so sick.

What I didn't realize then is that I wasn't going to want to talk to my mom about what I was worried about because it's *her* that I'm always worried about. So having a therapist that I can just pour everything out to is a relief.

She's not my first therapist, by the way. I should probably mention that I did not like the first therapist I went to. It was an old man who really reminded me of every therapist stereotype you see in the movies. He was like, "Tell me about your relationship with your mom and your dad." And then he'd ask, "And how does that make you feel?" after every single thing I said. It was a little bit funny, but I just didn't feel comfortable talking to him for real. So we kept looking, and we found a younger therapist that I like so much better.

She doesn't really tell me what to do or anything like that. She just helps me think through everything—she asks a lot of questions that kind of lead me to realize things on my own as I try to explain what I was thinking or feeling.

I'm pretty sure that I'll keep seeing her even when I go to college, if I'm able to. I think I should be able to since we do video therapy sessions.

It's like having someone whose purpose is to help you understand yourself, and then once you understand you feel so much better about your problems. I think it's because even if you can't fix and control everything, like I can't change my mom's cancer, but when you talk it out you can at least fix and control how you think about and deal with it.

Lindsey

The absolute best resource I have is my journaling. I took a creative writing summer camp class where we journaled sometimes, and I found it so calming.

So since then, I've made a bunch of journals. I've got a dream journal that I keep by my bedside so I can write down any dreams that I have right when I wake up before I forget them. I just started doing it because I have really vivid dreams, and then I realized I can kind of tell if I'm anxious about something when I'll dream something similar like I'm running away from something for a few nights in a row.

Then I have a different kind of dream journal, a "things I want to do" journal. I guess it's a "future plans" journal. Basically, it's like a Pinterest board in a notebook where I put all the traveling I want to do and colleges I'm interested in. Careers, stuff like that.

Then I have just the regular journal that I write about my day. I kind of spend more time on the future plans journal more than my regular one because it's more fun. If I'm really stressed out about my life, I might skip my regular journal completely and just pull out the future journal. When things are going wrong, I'd rather plan what I'm going to do one day and map out how I want my life to look. It's a really good outlet, I get to be creative and doodle, I fill it with pictures and notes, and I feel better when I'm done.

Lindsey uses multiple journals as an outlet for her stress. When she is especially stressed out, she journals about her plans for the future. *Illustration by Kate Haberer.*

ACTIVITY BREAK: FILTERING HUMOR
INTO SOCIAL DISTANCING

The nature of community has changed in light of COVID-19; we interact with others sometimes very differently than we did before. *Negative filtering* is an anxiety habit in which we can only see the negatives instead of the full, complex picture which includes both positive and negative qualities of a situation. It can be easy to think of social distancing and the potentially isolating nature of quarantining through negative filtering. This activity is not designed to minimize the difficulty of social isolation, but considers the other aspects in which it can be amusing or even surreally entertaining.

Take a few minutes to reflect on and consider the funny and interesting potential about the changes in physical and social distance and connecting to others solely via screens. What if we never realized our friends were a full foot taller or shorter than us? What if no one could tell that you were secretly a centaur (a mythological creature with the upper body of a human and lower body of a horse)? What if everyone's fake Zoom backgrounds were their real backgrounds and everyone really lived in castles, haunted houses, and magical schools? What other possibilities are there? Let your imagination run wild considering the amusing possibilities we might never notice when we interact online.

PART II
COPING WITH STRESS

CHAPTER FIVE

ON ANGER AND COPING WITH THE FIGHT RESPONSE

USEFUL ANGER AND PROBLEMS WITH MISPLACED AGGRESSION

Anxiety disorders and panic attacks appear to be the brain's fight-or-flight response misfiring. There *are* times when the fight-or-flight response is the best one—though modern circumstances have changed, we still need to physically defend ourselves or escape situations sometimes. However, most of the time we know that "fight" and "flight" behavior can lead us to ineffective habits that worsen chronic stress or develop into other disorders. In the following two chapters, we'll explore issues with anger, aggression, discomfort, and escapism.

A common issue with "fight" behavior that can lead to other severe life and relationship problems is misplaced aggression. Have we ever lost our tempers over something extremely minor? Sometimes we feel irritable or snap at someone when hungry or in pain. Does feeling humiliation sometimes provoke fury at those who witnessed it? When we yell at someone who didn't do anything wrong or we fly off the handle about something unimportant, we might be experiencing stressors, having a fight response, and then channeling our aggression toward innocent targets. The real source of our aggression is the stressor triggering our fight response, not what ended up being targeted. Furthermore, the emotion we feel might look like anger on the surface, but it might well be something else.

Ineffective coping through aggression can have an unhealthy ripple effect on our social relationships. Our family and friends can lash out at us and pass along those irritable feelings from their stress, and vice versa. Situations where we accept blame for someone else's hostility or mood as our responsibility can become toxic and even abusive very quickly. Recognizing that another stressor is provoking someone's mistreatment of us can help relieve confusion and self-blame, but should not justify or excuse abusive or toxic actions.

In these cases, identifying the true stressor can be surprisingly difficult if we don't pause to think before reacting. Remaining mindful about what's really bothering us can help us focus on what needs to be resolved instead of ineffectively diverting our attention and energy. Pause and consider what effect or outcome we desire before we act—acting on "fight" behavior can block the outcomes we *truly* want. For example, deep down we might desire comfort—a listening ear, understanding feedback, or a warm hug. Being sarcastic, rude, or yelling are counterproductive ways to get what we are seeking.

There are understanding individuals who can see past our aggression to the pain we're in or stress we're experiencing, but misplaced aggression can be isolating when we push away our support systems or turn that aggression inward toward ourselves with self-blame, self-loathing, and even acts of self-harm. Or we can create a self-fulfilling prophecy: we fear that we are unloved, feel angry at a stressor, lash out at others, and then take their rejection of our behavior as proof of our unlovability.

Note the difference between *aggression* and *anger*. In many cases, our upbringing and school environments teach us that feeling and/or expressing anger is inappropriate—that any feeling other than happiness should be hidden. However, this doesn't teach us to distinguish between a perfectly normal emotion (anger) and a problematic behavior (aggression). Anger can be a useful emotion. When we pay attention to when we feel it (without immediately acting on it), we can learn what sort of things we value most. Anger can be motivating, helping us to speak for ourselves and encouraging us to tackle our challenges and stressors. Alternatively, aggression is a hostile behavior, including actions like yelling, making threats, damaging property, and physically harming ourselves and others. The emotion we feel does not mean the associated behavior is required. If we must take action, there are non-aggressive outlets for that fight impulse, like writing an unsent letter or channeling that energy toward a good run or workout.

When we feel angry, this is a reminder to investigate the stressor and give ourselves permission to feel and express it in appropriate ways. Some psychologists describe anger as a "secondary emotion"— anger emerges as the second emotion covering up another feeling underneath, like sadness, fear, shock, humiliation, or disgust. What real goal, value, or concern does this feeling alert us to? When we can step out of our knee-jerk reactions, we create breathing room between the stressor, the emotions we have about it, and how we respond behavior-wise. In doing so, we can identify what we're really feeling, then respond in healthier, different ways instead of acting out feelings through destructive behaviors.[1]

As a secondary emotion, anger can serve as a protective shield. It can be the "safest" choice—yelling instead of crying, fury instead of lonely despair. Sometimes when we feel angry, that anger is protecting us from some painful feelings lurking underneath. That means we have to choose to be vulnerable, peek underneath the anger, and see what it covers. What stressor triggered our anger? Is there any other feeling we're avoiding or are unaware of underneath our anger? Why do those emotions feel less "safe" than anger? What part of ourselves is vulnerable if we admit what is beneath our anger?

Professor of social work Brené Brown reminds us that vulnerability is required to feel emotion, and that "[to] believe vulnerability is weakness is to believe that feeling is weakness. . . . Our rejection of vulnerability often stems from our associating it with emotions like fear, shame, grief, sadness, and disappointment—emotions we don't want to discuss, even when they profoundly affect the way we live, love, work, and even lead."[2] Even when we've been raised to avoid expressing anger and have been encouraged to only show happiness, other emotions are so personally intimate and raw that we would rather use anger instead. Letting anger overtake us into aggression, including pushing away our loved ones, can be a way to reject the risk of being vulnerable—where our true selves, emotions, and desires might be rejected. Without vulnerability, however, we also miss out on a full range of experiences including love, joy, and creativity.

Similarly, psychologist Susan David articulates neatly the freedom we can find in pausing, identifying, and naming our emotions clearly:

> Learning to label emotions with a more nuanced vocabulary can be absolutely transformative. People who can identify the full spectrum of emotion—who realize, how, for example, sadness differs from boredom, or pity, or loneliness, or nervousness—do much, much better at managing the ups and downs of ordinary existence than those who see everything in black and white.
>
> Along with the importance of precisely labeling our emotions comes the promise that once we do give them a name, our feelings can provide useful information. They signal rewards and dangers. They point us in the direction of our hurt. They can also tell us which situations to engage with and which to avoid. They can be beacons, not barriers, helping us identify what we most care about and motivating us to make positive changes.[3]

When David says that our feelings can "point us in the direction of our hurt," this our signal to identify the true underlying emotions motivating our feelings—often not anger at all, but something else.

For example, we might feel anger when a friend invites others to come over, but not us. Later we find out that everyone had a good time without us; maybe we find out by seeing pictures on social media featuring everyone laughing and enjoying themselves. We might feel anger; that anger might lead to aggression and a fight. But if we pause to identify the source of our anger, we find that it's really sadness, loneliness, and fear that we're not good enough or our friends are drifting from us. If we want to bridge the gap of our isolation and make better connections with our friends that we value, then aggression doesn't serve that purpose. When we can pause before reacting, we can align our inner lives with our outer actions.

ANGER
IN REVIEW

SUMMARY OF EVENT

When S. and I started dating, Will began acting really weird and possessive. He isn't my dad or my boyfriend. He says I'm being dramatic, but I'm not.

INITIAL EMOTIONAL RESPONSE

Angry that he told S about the time we went to Disney prove he knew more about me. SO ANGRY that he told S to go home when I was sick & didn't mention he visited.

UNDERLYING FEELINGS/VALUES

I feel embarrassed and disrespected. I'm not a toy for him to fight over. I can have friends who don't own me or try to control my decisions.

ACTION TAKEN

Told Will why I'm upset. Blocked him from seeing my posts because his comments are always weird, too.

NEXT TIME?

Speak up sooner. Will has been tearing S down and pretending like he has some claim on me for a while.

Keeping track of our anger using a chart like this can help determine the relationship between the initial emotional surge we feel and our true underlying emotions. Additionally, by evaluating how we responded and what we might consider doing next time, we give ourselves space between the emotion we felt, the behavior we took, and how we can improve the interaction in the future. Download a free blank version from the author's website at christiecognevich.com. *Illustration by Christie Cognevich.*

In a healthy friendship, we should be able to articulate to our friends that we felt hurt when we saw they had a good time together, and that we'd like to do something similar sometime. This requires vulnerability, but love is risk with great reward. If our friends aren't receptive to our honest and non-hostile communication, then we might have an unhealthy dynamic. It's worth evaluating the larger patterns in our relationships if we are consistently feeling hurt and not being heard when we communicate effectively—but evaluate them in the calm space between those emotions and our aggressive responses to them. Not every anger should lead to a fight, and not every feeling is rooted in fact.

Remember, avoiding aggression does not mean responding passively and accepting how we're treated. Anger can tell us when we're being used, disrespected, and/or hurt. There is a difference between standing up for ourselves assertively and healthily—without aggressive confrontation—and picking a fight.

In what ways have your family and friends helped you find healthier outlets for anger?

Cam

I'm a sore loser. I'm competitive. Really, my whole family is. You should not play any kind of game or sport with any of us.

I have a great friend named Katy who's our friend group's biggest cheerleader. She always remembers to make these big celebration posts on Instagram whenever it's a big game day or competition day for someone. Katy will show up at my soccer games with a big sign to cheer me on, or bake us all cookies for our birthdays. The thing about Katy is that she kind of thinks that we did great even when we didn't. It's impossible to be mad because I let someone score when she's losing her mind excited because of the other stuff I did that looked impressive to her.

I know there have been days when I was worried about how I'd been doing in practice, and then I saw Katy in the stands with her big sign screaming my name. She really helps motivate me to do my best and not get angry even when I don't win. Like even when I don't do well—our team lost a division championship game, and I played really badly that day—she still finds a way to make me laugh or feel better in the end.

Really, when I think about it, I think the difference between someone like Katy and my parents is that I don't feel like she's pressuring me to do better. She wants me to play well because she knows I love soccer, not for any other reason. My parents get mad at me when I don't do well, and I get mad right back at them. I'd rather have Katy cheering me on than anyone else in the world. I don't want to let her down by losing my temper, or yelling at her when I don't win. My parents, I'll definitely get an attitude with them if it goes badly.

John

I had a lot of anger when my dad died. A lot. I don't really know who or what I was angry about. At God, or at the world, or maybe just at my dad for not taking good care of his health and leaving us. I don't know.

My big brother was my role model. He put up with me when I was being a little jerk about everything, and he was always just so calm and understanding. He's three years older than me, and I can always count on him to help me when I need it. He's my family, but he's also my friend. When our dad died, I was a freshman and he was a senior. Our mom had to start working more to make ends meet, and my brother just really helped me a lot in getting through the hardest parts dealing with our dad being gone.

For example, our mom couldn't always cook like she used to because either she was working or she was really tired. And that made me mad, too. Not at her, just that she had to experience that.

But my brother just started watching cooking videos on YouTube or Buzzfeed and making stuff. He would do things like sing and dance in the kitchen to make me laugh while he was doing it. I look back now, and I realize that whole year he made sure we got to keep some things normal, that he made it look light and fun even when it was work.

When he went to college, I kept calling him with stupid questions about how to make spaghetti or boil eggs. He never got annoyed with me or anything. He just sent me links to his favorite videos and recipes and answered my questions. Now I can actually cook really well, and I think I learned a lot just watching him. Really, I learned about dealing with the anger, plus how to cook. How to love my family and stick with them through the hard times.

Leila

I used to say that I'm just an angry person. I feel so spiky all the time, if that makes sense. In every direction, spikes. I just want people to stay away sometimes.

My boyfriend is a very chill person. He always says, "don't get angry, get even." And he's so laid back, so I'd always laugh and be like, "Okay, you're the last person in the world I could see getting revenge." I'd laugh every time he said that.

A few months ago, I finally asked him what he means when he says "get even," and he was like, "You know, things that are even are nice and orderly and neat. All the corners and sides are lined up and even. So instead of being messy about something, go clean your house. Go fix stuff instead of breaking stuff." Which, I have to admit, is a pretty good philosophy.

I've been thinking about that lately. Making things even not as revenge, but as a way of making my life or the world a little better.

Jenna

Truthfully, I think my parents have kind of shown me how to *not* act in anger by being awful to each other. Like, watching them shows how I want my future relationship with someone to be different.

A year ago, I would have said I have just a normal family. We're pretty happy. Sometimes there are problems, but nothing major. My dad worked in the restaurant business, so that took a big hit with the pandemic. At first, I guess he just thought he'd be

Due to the pandemic, Jenna's father loses his job. Meanwhile, her mother starts working from home. The situation leads to her parents constantly fighting, and Jenna feels uncomfortable in her own home. *Illustration by Kate Haberer.*

home for a couple weeks then things would go back to normal, but then the restaurant decided to close for good. My mom started working from home.

Maybe it's just that the house isn't that big, or maybe we just got sick of each other. I don't know. But I started hearing them fighting all the time about stupid stuff. Dad keeps walking around in the background when Mom's on a video call. Dad didn't let the dog out and now he's barking while Mom's working.

At first, I was kind of mad at my mom. Like, cut him a break. He just lost his job, he's upset. Then it was like, is he *trying* to upset her? Is he mad that she still has a job and he doesn't? There's no way he's walking around in pajama pants when she's on an important call by accident. She'll tell us her exact schedule so we know when to stay quiet, and he'll barge in and try to talk to her exactly when she said not to. There's no way it's a coincidence. He's like a big sad kid who needs attention all the time.

They've just become really petty and childish with each other. She yells, and he's sarcastic. She slams the door closed, and he still stomps around making noise. It's hard to blame my mom for being so mad after months of this. So, they've been a terrible example, but I know I want something different in my life.

ACTIVITY BREAK: REIMAGINING ANGER

What if, much like in the Pixar film *Inside Out*, our anger was a person? What are its hopes and fears? What is it seeking? What is it reacting to? What sort of things does it want to tell us, and what do we want to tell it?

Now take a few minutes to compose a "Dear Anger" letter in your head. Would you want to tell Anger thank you for showing you when you aren't being treated well? Would you want to tell Anger to take a vacation for a while? Or you can even consider what you would tell other people's anger.

CHAPTER SIX

ON DISCOMFORT
AND COPING WITH
THE FLIGHT RESPONSE

USEFUL DISCOMFORT AND PROBLEMS
WITH FORGIVENESS AND LETTING GO

Much like the problem with the "fight" response, when unpacking issues with the "flight" response, we have to distinguish between feeling our emotions and acting with ineffective behaviors. In many cases, a stressor provokes uncomfortable emotions: perhaps anger, sadness, fear, shock, contempt, or disgust. It is not unreasonable to be inclined to escape these discomforts.

There comes a time when we let things go. That time doesn't have to be on any specific timetable. Depending on the issue and the person affected, it may take weeks, months, years.

Just like many of us have been taught inappropriately that anger is "bad," many of us have been taught that showing emotions other than joy is a sign of weakness or will make us a burden. Just like with the fight response, resist the urge to avoid these feelings. Simply feel them for a while, even if unpleasant. No feeling is "bad"; we can learn much about ourselves from these emotions before we make any choices or take any actions at all. Why are we feeling this way? What did this event or person mean to us that it provoked us to feel this way? Explore our emotion's purpose *before* setting it aside.

Yes, this might hurt and be difficult. With practice, we can get better sitting in our most painful emotional states—observing them, asking questions of them, learning about ourselves through them. Though it may seem obvious, discomfort is by definition not a comfortable state to remain in, so it does require effort. At its worst, the flight response puts pressure on us to hide our feelings from ourselves and others because they can be messy, ugly, uncomfortable. Acknowledging our suffering hurts. We fix the source of our discomfort by forcing easy resolutions that are really just avoidance. Additionally, the people who love us might struggle with watching us experience that emotional discomfort. Watching us in pain might hurt them, and in turn we might feel rejected and invalidated when they urge "letting go" or "moving on."

"Letting go" and "moving on" are fine concepts in theory. In practice, however, we can be pressured to toss aside meaningful sorrows we're still in the process of working through and grieving over. We can take our time with sadness, anger, and fear. In fact, we *don't* have to move to let it go as quickly as possible. There is a difference between productive anger that teaches us who can and can't be trusted, that helps motivate and empower us to protect ourselves, and dwelling in rage. We can be pushed to "forgive and forget" behaviors that we might not have finished processing and healing from—sweeping abusive or toxic practices under the rug in the name of forgiveness, which over the long term enables harmful people to hurt us or others again. Be careful of the pressure, both from within ourselves and from others, to forgive; it can be a form of avoidance. We might hide our problems, thinking we're helping ourselves move on, when in fact we haven't actually addressed or repaired our wounds, but only suppressed them.

In addition to the pressure to "let go," there are other ways to escape our emotional truth in unhealthy ways. While our ancient human ancestors might have literally run away from physical threats, a common contemporary escape is in figurative rather than literal flights. We can numb ourselves in ways that include social withdrawal and substance use.[1] All too often, we embrace escape through alcohol, drugs, food, sex, shopping, internet usage, video games, and other forms of self-medicating. Additionally, we don't always need substances to run from our problems. We might avoid difficult discussions, dodge texts and phone calls from people we aren't ready to face, or put off big projects that make us feel anxious. However, running away from what we are thinking and feeling means only that we ultimately lose a part of ourselves when we can't identify our emotions or reveal the true concerns beneath them. Social withdrawal, self-medicating, and otherwise avoiding, ignoring, suppressing, procrastinating, delaying, and pretending problems away are *not* coping strategies for stress. They are all ways to prevent ourselves from actively dealing with our issues.

There *are* healthy flights. In the case of a bad breakup, we might choose to delete all of our social media pictures with our ex so that we can have closure as we turn the pages on that life chapter and ensure that we can avoid continually seeing painful reminders of better times. This social media cleanse is a way of closing the past and walking away, looking forward with a clean slate. This action may cause us tremendous sadness and anger as we go through our feed and choose which photos to delete, but it deals with the issue directly by grieving and closing that chapter.

Temporary flight as a means of calming ourselves can be extremely effective. Taking a walk to calm down before tackling a difficult task is effective. Mentally retreating for a few moments—to breathe, do counting exercises, or other stress-relief exercises—is also effective. If we know we're going to have a difficult conversation with someone (such as talking to a significant other about relationship problems, or discussing college finances with our parents), then we can decide together— in advance—to pause the discussion for five or ten minutes when we need to take a break before anyone becomes too upset to communicate effectively. Getting up in the middle of an argument, running out, and slamming the door is far less effective.

There is a difference between coping and escaping. There is even a difference between a temporary escape—taking a break from difficulty before returning to it—and avoiding ever dealing with the issue until it erupts in our faces. This book, for example, provides brief "brain break" activities at the end of each chapter, usually designed to be lighthearted in nature as a shift from the heavy emotional lifting beforehand. Notice

WEEK
OF
11/14-11/20

DISCOMFORT
IN REVIEW

- fight with mom

- ran into Andy out with Amy when they said they didn't have any plans for the night.

- later saw them post on IG together with Olivia and I haven't seen her in weeks

THIS WEEK'S
STRESSORS

- with mom, just so angry I could feel my face burning.

- with Andy and Amy, my heart was skipping beats and I could feel my pulse in my wrists. Chest felt tight.

- similar with IG. Heartbeat fluttered a little, tight chest. A little milder this time.

PHYSICAL
SENSATIONS

- Mom is so much harder on me than she is on Luke.

- I wish she would just pay attention to him and ignore me if I can't do anything right.

- I messed up the gov't project because my part was late. Probably Andy & Amy are mad about that. I guess I deserve being left out anyway.

UNCOMFORTABLE
THOUGHTS

- Slammed door on mom, didn't feel better. She asked if we could talk after dinner. Felt better after talking, but still a little upset.

- Told Andy and Amy hi. Acted normal, like I didn't care. Cried in the car driving home, took the long way back. Ignored the IG story.

HOW I
RESPONDED

When we are struggling with stress, it can be difficult to notice our physical symptoms, thought patterns, and how we're reacting in the moment. Familiarizing ourselves with our own discomfort can help us recognize when we're approaching an unhealthy state or improve our responses later. Download a free blank version of this chart from the author's website at christiecognevich.com. *Illustration by Christie Cognevich.*

these activities range from a few minutes to ten minutes. Self-care is allowing ourselves to rest and recharge our emotional reserves with the recognition that we then return to our tasks feeling renewed.

As much as we sometimes want to, we cannot "kill off" our own feelings without doing harm to ourselves. One common way we try to mentally escape without the use of substances is by bottling up our feelings or replacing them with forced positivity. As psychiatrist Susan David describes it, a "bottler" of emotions tends to resist or smother their emotions because those feelings cause discomfort or "they think that being anything less than bright and chipper is a sign of weakness."[2] When forcing ourselves to only think positively, we deny our emotional truths and fall out of touch with our needs, goals, and values. Ultimately, "attempting to minimize or ignore thoughts and emotions only serves to amplify them" when they emerge at unexpected times and cause more distress.[3]

What are some ways you or someone you love has struggled with "flight" behavior, avoidance, and escapism?

Cam

My mom isn't in the picture and my dad has a drinking problem, so sometimes I have to be more of the parent. I know he's just trying to escape whatever his issues are, but the issue is the drinking itself. The escape is the problem.

That becomes hard for me because I think that anyone who has a family member with a lot of problems can relate to how easy it is to prioritize their needs over your own. I'm not saying that it's a terrible thing to love someone who has issues. He's not always drunk, and he does try really hard to be there for me. It's also true that he isn't always there for me even if he wants to be.

I used to think when I was really little that it was my fault he drank so much. If I did things right, he wouldn't get upset and have a drink. Or if I made him happy he wouldn't drink. When I was really little, like maybe only four, I'd try to do things to make him smile. Draw him a picture, try to clean up my toys more. Anything I could think of to help out so that he would be happy and not drink. Obviously, I didn't really understand that alcoholism and addiction are diseases, and it's nothing I did or can do to fix it.

I try to keep track and remind him when he has appointments. I do a lot of the errands. After school I get the groceries or pick up his medication at the pharmacy so that I never have to worry about him drinking and driving. In our state you can get a driver's permit at fifteen if a licensed driver rides with you, so I got mine right after my birthday so that I could help out more. I don't think he would drink and drive, and as far as I know he hasn't, but it was something I used to worry about a lot.

The biggest difficulty I've had lately is that it's almost time for me to make some college decisions, and I worry about leaving my dad behind. There are some colleges I'm interested in that are out of state, and at first I wasn't going to apply because I know my dad needs me here. My grandparents got pretty upset about that, and my grandpa insisted I apply to all of them. He called my dad and talked to him about it, too. He and I don't talk about his drinking that much—it's kind of the elephant in the room—but after my grandpa called, my dad came in to talk to me about it. Basically, he agreed with my grandpa that I should make my decision for my future even if it means leaving the state.

That was a huge relief, like a big weight off my chest, when he said that.

John

I worry a lot about my aunt, my mom's younger sister. She and I are really close, and she's a funny and wonderful person. She has some mental health issues that make me really stressed that she might hurt herself. She has depression and an addictive personality, so she really struggles with food, alcohol, and drugs as her escape. She had to take some prescription pills when she was younger, and then she just started taking them when she wasn't supposed to. From there it just got worse and worse. She describes it as anything that makes her feel better she'll eat or drink until it makes her feel *terrible*.

When she's in a bad place, sometimes she just says things like, "I hate myself so much, I wish I could die." Our family helps her get into rehab when things get like that for her. I've lost count of how many times she's done rehab, but I feel so sick every time it happens because there's nothing I can do but wait and see how she's doing. My mom always says the only thing we can do is love her and listen when she needs to talk.

My family is really open about sharing serious stuff like this, so I've been aware of my aunt's problems probably since elementary school. I'm glad my family has been so open, because I think people say stupid and judgmental things about stuff they don't know anything about. Things they're afraid of, even if they don't want to admit it. Maybe I would have said stupid and hurtful things around my aunt if I hadn't known better. And I think knowing what's really going on with her, even though it's stressful sometimes, has made me a better and more understanding person in general. I know a lot of people who are so judgy about addiction, even though it's really common. My friends have said really awful, stupid things about "junkies" and "crackheads" and they don't even know that my aunt—whom they think is really cool, because she *is*—has an addiction problem.

It wasn't her fault she got prescribed the meds when she was younger. She has a lot of issues she's working through. Addiction is both her escape and her problem.

I wish I could make rehab work for her better, because it works for a little while where she'll come out looking and sounding much better. That will last for a few months or sometimes a year. But then she'll have a bad breakup or lose her job, she'll cope in the wrong way, and it all goes downhill for her again.

Rachel

My mom has always struggled with substance abuse, and eventually my dad left and took me with him. When I was really little, there were days and weeks where she would just disappear, and I never really understood where she was. My dad or grandparents would just say she wasn't feeling well or she needed a little vacation. Eventually, I realized that wasn't normal, and at that point she was in and out of my life randomly. You just never knew if she was going to show up or not.

The summer before my freshman year, I got a call from my little sister asking if she could come over because our mom was gone. She has a different dad, so she didn't live with me. I had this weird, really bad feeling. Mom was always going off, but it sounded like something was really wrong this time. When my little sister showed up, it turned out that our mom had gotten arrested weeks ago for missing some important legal paperwork or a court date of some kind. My little sister had just been staying alone with our mom's random boyfriend at the time.

So then my little sister would have nightmares every night, and I'd just hold her till she calmed down and went back to sleep. At that point, I was really upset with my mom. It was like, you're supposed to be the one taking care of us. You're supposed to be a good example. How can you just do something irresponsible and go to jail, and not think about how that's going to affect your kids? How can you not realize what you're doing when you're never there for us so we have to take care of ourselves?

At the same time, I wasn't surprised. It's not the first time my mom has done something like that to really put us in danger. I remember one night when I was a lot younger, my little sister and I were in the car with mom driving, going to the store. We were driving along, but I kept feeling my body jerk forward every few seconds. I don't know what my mom was on, but she kept nodding off at the wheel. Actually, what I remember thinking at the time was that my dad was going to be so mad if he found out. At some point we were weaving around side streets with mom nodding off when cop lights started flashing blue and red. I remember her sitting up straighter and waking up more, yelling at us to calm down. I guess we were crying, and she was trying to act like everything was fine.

My mom is out of jail now, but I know she's just not trust-worthy or reliable. She runs from her problems. I've had to be a lot more responsible because I refuse to be like her. There's a lot of stress sometimes worrying that I'll be like her and run from my problems instead of trying to solve them. But I always want to be there for my little sister, be there for her in a way that my mom never was to me.

Alivia

Well, when I was born, my mom wanted a girly girl. And she wanted her to be smart and popular and pretty. From the very beginning, it was very obvious that the things that people just naturally pick up on socially just didn't come naturally to me. Good kids aren't supposed to interrupt choir practice to tell the teacher, "I know all the lyrics." They aren't supposed to wander into someone else's conversation to say "hey!" And I just struggled to figure that out, so I got made fun of a lot.

When I was really young, my mom just decided I was choosing to be awkward on purpose. I'm not sure where she got that from, but on a daily basis she would sit me down and yell about why I was choosing to be such a weird kid and how I was doing this and no one liked me. Maybe it was supposed to be motivating? It wasn't.

So, I started drinking at age fourteen. I was extremely alone with an abusive mother and my dad never wanted to make waves. My mom is such a controlling person that she picks his clothes out for him and their schedule and exactly what they do, and he goes along with it. "Pick your battles," he always says. I don't think my dad really understood why I didn't just do that, why I always made trouble somehow, but it was mainly just that the things that bothered my mother about me were inherent. They weren't things I could change. It was just me being myself, socially awkward, bullied, with ADHD, that she objected to.

With my mom, I felt like I could never let my guard down. That meant at school I had to pretend I was okay, too. I was being bullied, I couldn't let my mom know, and I felt like the first rule

of bullies was don't let them smell blood in the water. So everything had to look like it was fine from the outside. Drinking helped
because it made it easier to pretend I really *was* what I acted like.

I had my first drink, and it was anesthesia. I *had* to be there
with my mother living in her house. I couldn't get away. But when
I drank, sometimes even just the stress of having to make sure I
was behaving normally while drunk was somehow *less* stressful
than living under her eye and criticism and abuse. It was, at first,
the lesser of two stressors because I had this set, achievable goal.
There was this checklist: don't act drunk, don't slur, don't trip, don't
let them smell your breath. That's an easier checklist than acting
normal. Like, what is normal?

So if I could focus on pretending I wasn't drunk, I didn't have
to think about all the other stuff I didn't want to address. That
didn't make it go away. It made a lot of things worse. But when I
was fourteen, it seemed like my only way of dealing with my mom.
It wasn't until I got to college that I even learned there were people
who did like me.

You know that advice that adults always tell teenagers, that it'll
get better someday? Like, sure, sure. But I wish I really could have
convinced my younger self of that. That there is a point where you
get to make your decisions and control your life more, and that's
when it does get better.

**Have you ever felt pressured to "let it go" or "forgive and
forget"? Is there a way to hold onto your experiences, however
painful, without letting them destroy you?**

Alivia

I don't communicate with my mother anymore. I don't want to
forget that she was physically, verbally, and emotionally abusive. I
can't forgive that or allow it to be "acceptable" because I decided to
let it go.

Honestly, one of my deepest wishes is that my dad outlives her, so that I can actually have a relationship with him. As far as I can tell, he and I are actually pretty similar as people. But now that I'm no longer in their house and I can look back, I realize that I don't know him very well at all. And—as offended as he'd probably be to hear this—I don't think he actually knows me (in any real way) at all. I would love to change that. But as long as my mom is alive, it's impossible. If his condition for being in my life is that my mom has to be in my life, then I can't enable his enabling her.

But at the end of the day, it's fine that I don't have a connection with my biological family. My found family of friends is just as valuable—maybe even more so because we chose each other on purpose. At some point, I had to stop bashing my head against what I can't have, and start acknowledging the invaluable preciousness of what I found all by myself. My friends are more family than blood.

Once I accepted that, I don't sit around thinking about my mom or how angry or hurt I am with her. Not forgiving her is important, but it doesn't mean I'm burning with rage or thinking about it all the time. I'm just not letting people pressure me into talking to her, seeing her, anything like that. I don't need or want an apology from her. We will not have a relationship, period.

I think that's why people always *think* you have to forgive and forget. They think that if you don't forgive, it just burns in you, cutting into your soul or something. That if you don't forgive, if you don't forget, you're angry all the time. I'm not. I'm protecting myself from someone who did real harm. That feels *good*, not bad.

Anna

My boyfriend and I were together for three years, and then he broke up with me. He wanted me to quit drama or dance since they take up so much of my time. He and I were together since we were twelve, and I've been in dance since I was three and doing theater since I was ten, so he knew that performing is important to me. It wasn't a new thing I'd just picked up.

In the end he was just so unsupportive. He wouldn't ask how my practice went, he'd just be like, "So are you going to quit soon?" He refused to go to one of my performances because he went to the one last year.

And if we didn't spend much time together then maybe I should have been like, okay, it's true, I don't have time for a relationship. I'm neglecting him. But I saw him all the time and we spent basically every weekend together. He never actually asked if we could spend more time together, either, just was like, "you need to quit."

When we broke up, he told everyone I cared more about myself than him. You know what? Isn't that how it's supposed to be, shouldn't I care about myself and what makes me happy? If he doesn't make me feel good or supported, then why should he stay in my life? I'm not going to change my passions because he demands it.

Two weeks later he apologized and asked me to forgive him and take him back. My friends thought I was crazy when I said no. They were like, "you need to forgive him." I miss him, but he really hurt me. You don't spend three years with someone and talk about how much you love them, then demand they give up something they love.

Maybe I'll change my mind, but I think I made the right choice. Because I'm still not giving up dance or drama. The problem is still going to be there, and I'm still hurt that he acted like that. I can still love him and not forgive him.

ACTIVITY BREAK: JOY PARK CENTRAL

This chapter was all about discomfort; our activity is all about joy. Imagine there is a theme park specifically designed for your delight. Would it be indoors or outdoors, sunny or dim, warm or cool? What kind of adventures would you have—rollercoasters or escape rooms or fun restaurants? Would you reinterpret "adventure" to mean a huge library of adventure books and not literal adventures? What kinds of rest areas would be there, and how many people would be there? Would there be a hotel attached, and what would it be like for your comfort? What would be the ideal amount of time for a visit, and how many things would there be to do? Would you design it for a younger version of yourself, or yourself now? Take into consideration your limits and what makes you feel overwhelmed. Take a few minutes to think about how this park would be custom tailored into the Goldilocks perfect fit for your enjoyment.

CHAPTER SEVEN

EFFECTIVE COPING THROUGH COMMUNITY

THE TEND-AND-BEFRIEND RESPONSE AND BUILDING CONNECTION

We've talked about the drawbacks to the fight-or-flight response when dealing with modern concerns. Overall, the tend-and-befriend stress response, which motivates us to seek out supportive communities, can be a more effective impulse. Having a community and connecting with others—feeling seen and wanted, and having a sense of belonging—provides stress relief and health benefits.

Brené Brown says that after decades of research and earning her doctorate in social work, she has learned for certain that "[c]onnection is why we're here. We are hardwired to connect with others, it's what gives purpose and meaning to our lives, and without it there is suffering."[1] The tend-and-befriend stress response can be an effective antidote to the weariness of being stressed and burned out. Still, we must remain mindful of some difficulties related to our social cravings—such as reaching out to a toxic friend who reinforces pain instead of healing, or struggling with the frustration of extreme social isolation.

Certainly, the COVID-19 pandemic has demonstrated how difficult it can be to overcome social disconnects. Many feel the need for social bonding as comfort, even introverts. Loneliness can complicate other stressors, adding insult to injury. We know that social fulfillment positively impacts physical and mental health, whereas isolation leads to the opposite. A CDC study showed that after three months of quarantine, as a result of the extreme isolation, "about 40% of U.S. adults were

89

reporting at least one mental health or substance use concern. When it came to young adults aged 18–24, that number jumped to nearly 75%."[2] Even if we aren't at a crisis point at a given time, stress can grind us down without a supportive community at our backs.

One problem is that reaching out in itself can be stressful. When we have stress about our stress, anxiety about our anxiety, we might feel helpless to act without worsening our situation. This can seem like an impossible paralysis cycle to break, especially for those with social anxiety.

Social anxiety is different than introversion, which is a personality trait. Instead, social anxiety, like other anxiety disorders, is measured by fear and its negative impact on our relationships and lives. Individuals with social anxiety experience worry during social interactions and while in the presence of others (whether simply being observed while engaging in normal activities or while giving a speech or performance). Additionally, individuals with social anxiety live in fear of judgment by others. In response, we might suffer through social interactions or avoid them altogether.[3]

If sharing ourselves and our passions with others seems overwhelming, then thinking about why we might have mental barriers in place is the first step to lowering them. Have we experienced invalidation from adults before? Are we worried about not being taken seriously? When and where did we learn these habits of keeping to ourselves without reaching out? Where and when did we learn shame about how we're feeling, about our interests and values? Identifying those reasons and concerns can help work around them.

Like most things, sharing ourselves with others is so much easier said than done. This is especially true when stressed or struggling with anxiety disorders. We can talk ourselves out of seeking friendship and support, especially when we need it most. If what we have to discuss is largely rooted in our problems, sometimes it's easier for us to turn inward and avoid others. Maybe we downplay our problems. Maybe we tell ourselves we have no one to trust, that no one cares, or that we're making a big deal over nothing. Maybe we worry that we're making too much trouble for our loved ones, and we put their needs first over ours. Maybe we feel angry at the world because we've tried to get help in our own way, but no one has helped. Maybe we feel afraid of judgment or rejection. Most people feel this way at times.

It is extremely difficult to unlearn anxious patterns that have allowed us to stay small and silent. If we grew up in an abusive household, we might have learned to take care of someone else's needs before our own and minimize our own problems. We might have avoided our parents completely, staying out of the way as a way of staying safe. The same goes for being bullied or struggling socially with our peers; we might have learned to curl into ourselves as a way to survive. Speaking to someone about our problems might run counter to the lesson we learned—that being quiet is the safest path. However, in this case, the habits we learned to protect ourselves are no longer benefiting us and might be hurting us instead.

Unfortunately, we *do* have to unlearn habits that no longer serve us and lower some of these mental barriers to create change in our lives. Excessive stress produces fear, but fear is just a worry, not a guarantee or predictor of bad things happening. Once we can identify our fears as nothing more than thoughts that we can let go, it becomes easier to not act on them or let them hold us back. This can take time and conscious effort; keep trying.

There are many ways to build ourselves up to make a change in the face of fear. We can create a motivating playlist and listen to it before doing something difficult. We can "armor up" in an outfit or look that makes us feel empowered, strong, smart, or beautiful—our favorite shirt or hat or the big jacket or the cool boots or our signature makeup that puts a spring in our step or fire in our spirit. Let the physical transformation seep into our mental patterns. Even something as simple as getting a good night's sleep, having a healthy breakfast, or taking a hot refreshing shower can reset our bodies and make us feel that much stronger to face the day's challenges.

The next step is building connections to others. This is practice for growing comfortable with talking honestly about our experiences, values, and more. Perhaps one of the most difficult steps in managing uncontrolled stress or anxiety is speaking about it for the first time. While others might already recognize that we have been struggling, they may not understand how much, in what ways, or why. We don't have to necessarily begin by talking about our struggles; simply reaching out to others to talk in general terms is the first step.

Remember that finding a "community" as part of the tend-and-befriend response doesn't specifically have to mean people we know in person. If we don't feel comfortable or safe yet with talking to others in person, there are alternatives like starting with talking to others in a supportive online community of peers with shared interests. Some of the most rewarding relationships can be with others who share our passion and enthusiasm. We may never even speak of personal matters, only about those hobbies and interests we mutually enjoy, and still receive tremendous health benefits from the healthy, rewarding interaction. The initial goal is simple connection, not necessarily confiding secrets, worries, or painful experiences. The rest can come later.

Animals are part of our community as well. If we receive gratification from connecting with animals, don't forget that spending time with our pets or friends' pets can be just as rewarding to our brain as human interaction. Volunteering at an animal shelter or helping others with their animals can be a highly rewarding source of dopamine for stress relief and a sense of well-being.

In short, the tend-and-befriend response can be one of the most useful ways to combat stress in our everyday lives and minimize the effects of chronic stress. Spending quality time with ourselves, as well as the people and animals we love and trust, can build the feeling of well-being and resilience to combat stress and anxiety. If these aren't people we trust to engage in honest conversations about our values, goals, and needs, then perhaps they are best kept as acquaintances or are not healthy additions to our lives at all. Feeling safe is first and foremost in embracing a healthy turn toward friends, family, and peers.

In what ways are you part of a community?

Anna

My passion is drama. I want to be an actress one day. I want to act in television and movies, but there's a huge amount of people in my life who have said, "We're supporting you, but we just want you to know this is a really hard career path, and . . . you're probably going to end up just working at Starbucks."

It's hard, because the theater and drama community is my life. They make me laugh, and I spend hours with them every single day, rehearsing three or four hours a day. Even when I didn't have a role, I did lights or wardrobe or makeup so I was there. Anyone who's done drama knows how it takes over your life. There's no other community and no other support like it. It's also so stressful.

Like, my first role, it was really minor. I had maybe a sentence to say. But I spent most of my time in rehearsals watching everyone else's performance and thinking they're better than me. No wonder they got bigger parts. So, I spend three hours after school there rehearsing, then I go home and still have to do my homework. The load is overwhelming, and that adds to the stress too. I don't think I enjoyed that first performance at all. It wasn't exciting, it was awful.

But I got past that. There's never been a time that I've been so stressed about it that I changed my mind. My mom initially wanted to be a makeup artist for theater and movies. She wanted to go to a school for that out of state, but my Maw Maw didn't want her to leave home and she never got to follow that dream. She ended up being happy in her chosen career—nursing—but that's what her mom did, too. That's a huge jump, from makeup artist to nursing. For a while, when I was around ten, I wanted to be a nurse, too.

Lately, I've realized that I just really want to stick to what I love. They're my community, my people, and this is what makes me feel most alive.

Anna spends most of her time at school play rehearsals comparing herself to her classmates' performances, making what should have been an exciting experience a stressful one. *Illustration by Kate Haberer.*

Lindsey

My family is so supportive, and they're my community. They support me, I support them. My little brother is moderately autistic. I'm not ashamed, and it's not his fault. I love him to death, and part of loving him is that I worry because he struggles with sensory processing disorders. Things like an itchy shirt or loud noises are super stressful for him. I don't always know what's bothering him, so I can't fix it.

I would do anything for him. I take being his big sister seriously. Like, just trying to be more aware of what he's experiencing so I can make sure I don't take him anywhere where I might put him in any overwhelming situations. I wouldn't make friends with anyone who is rude about anyone with special needs.

For people who aren't familiar with autism, one of the things he does to cope with being overwhelmed is called stimming. It's basically any kind of repetitive habit like rocking or flapping his hands to help calm or distract him. He does a few different things, so I try to check if he's stimming more than normal and make sure that he's comfortable. He likes chewing gum because the chewing helps, so I'll keep gum with me if he needs it.

We all try to make sure that we check out anything first before he does it or any place before we bring him. Like, my mom doesn't take him to the grocery store on football game days because the store plays the game really loudly over the speakers. It hurts my ears, actually, how loud they have it on, so I know he wouldn't be able to handle the volume. Any restaurant or place that has walls of televisions or stuff like that, it's just too much visual stuff, and he gets overwhelmed.

FINDING COMMUNITY AS A SENSITIVE OR INTROVERTED INDIVIDUAL

Introversion and sensitivity are not disorders, nor do these qualities necessarily have anything to do with having social anxiety. In encouraging the tend-and-befriend response, this book in no way suggests that introversion and sensitivity are traits to be "outgrown," "overcome," or otherwise changed. There is no requirement for our personal communities to be large, or for our socializing to occur in frequent or extended doses. Small one-on-one sessions with a handful of close relationships can provide equal reward for those who are inclined to smaller, quieter interactions. We can embrace our natural traits without having to change them and still find community.

Furthermore, if external social interactions tend to be draining, remember also that *we ourselves are the foundation of our own community*. We are our own first support system; we can begin talking to ourselves through journaling. Especially during the pandemic, as social anxiety rises, journaling can be an excellent outlet for self-expression that has real health benefits. Studies show that young adults who spent fifteen minutes a day journaling or drawing about a stressful event benefited from reduced anxiety and depression, even though the majority did not journal specifically about their feelings. Other studies have revealed that individuals who journal regularly see an immune system boost.[4] And ultimately, there is value in self-expression and articulating our own goals, values, concerns, and issues in different ways to ourselves before we share to family, friends, and others in our community.

In fact, a relentless societal pressure toward extroversion as a cultural ideal can itself be stressful and stigmatizing for introverts and sensitive individuals. Therefore, it's worth acknowledging and celebrating that a small but significant portion of the population (about 20 percent) is what psychotherapist Elaine N. Aron terms "highly sensitive."[5] Though we may represent a small segment of the overall population, the highly sensitive person (HSP) does not have a disorder, nor is high sensitivity the same as shyness or introversion (although it includes some of those traits). Sensitivity as a trait does not seem to exist on a spectrum; studies reveal that most people are sharply divided, and either we are or aren't highly sensitive.

Many HSPs have never seen our experiences recognized and celebrated as part of a larger community of people who share this trait. We are not alone. Our experiences with this temperament are identifiable and measured in four tendencies: depth of processing, overstimulation, emotional reactivity, and sensing subtleties. Through these four tendencies, HSPs "simply process everything more, relating and comparing what [we] notice to their past experience with other things," whether consciously or not—and this careful consideration means we are deeply inside our heads, noticing and feeling.[6]

This kind of sensitivity is hardwired into the brain and nervous system; HSP nervous systems seem "designed to react to subtle experiences" and are attuned to fine-motor movements, stillness, and more creative, synthesizing thought patterns.[7] Because HSPs take in so much information and are so sensitive to our environment, we can burn out easily, tending to avoid crowds and turn inward. This does leave us vulnerable to stress and social isolation. Being aware of what kinds of struggles we may face can help prepare for those issues. But in fact, sensitive individuals can overcome stressful situations quickly once they're familiar: "[w]hen sensitive individuals see right away that their situation is like a past one, thanks to having learned so thoroughly from thinking over that last time, we can react to a danger or opportunity faster than others."[8]

However, as part of our sensitivity, we are also powerfully moved by emotions (both positive and negative), are imaginative and creative, possess insights from our extended processing (which later helps us act intuitively and more quickly than others in similar situations we've already experienced), and have deep empathy for others. Given this rich inner life and complex processing, a disproportionate number of humanitarians—philosophers, historians, artists, readers, and writers, among others—are, in fact, highly sensitive.[9]

There are also many introverts who struggle to find our place in the world. We live in a culture that by and large loves to celebrate loud, extroverted individuals. We see a lot of variations on the typical extroverted action hero woven in our cultural fabric, a hero that fits what Susan Cain refers to as "the Extrovert Ideal" in her book *Quiet: The Power of Introverts in a World That Can't Stop Talking.* These individuals "[prefer] action to contemplation, risk-taking to heed-taking, certainty to doubt . . . [favor] quick decisions even at the risk of being wrong . . . [work] well in teams and [socialize] in groups."[10] Cain's theories follow cultural anthropologist Margaret Mead's suggestion that cultures value individual temperaments, and then "[embody] this choice in every thread of the social fabric—in the care of the young child, the games the children play, the songs the people sing, the structure of political organization, the religious observance, the art and the philosophy."[11] This social ideal may vary according to age, gender, social class, or occupation, among other categories. In China, studies show that quiet, sensitive children are highly valued and are "among those most chosen by others to be friends or playmates," and in Mandarin Chinese, the word "sensitive" has complimentary connotations.[12]

However, Western cultures tend to covet the outward-facing, action-loving extrovert, and this message is conveyed early in life through our storytelling. In the United States and Canada, several studies show a childhood preference for outgoing, exuberant, action-based "rough-and-tumble play" that is strongly correlated with positive parent, teacher, and peer evaluations of a child's competence and popularity.[13] As Cain points out, "We're told that to be great is to be bold, to be happy is to be sociable."[14]

And yet, despite this pressure, remember that "one third to one half of Americans are introverts. . . . Given that the United States is among the most extroverted of nations, the number must be at least as high in other parts of the world."[15] When Cain argues that we broadcast extroversion as a social ideal in our cultural fabric, it's worth considering how we might tell ourselves stories about our introversion or quietness being weird, when in fact there is nothing wrong with our temperament or traits. Introversion is not shyness or any kind of social disorder. As Cain points out, there are countless definitions of introversion and extroversion, but one way of describing the traits is that introverts simply "focus on the meaning [we] make of the events swirling around [us]; extroverts plunge into the events."[16]

Regardless of whether we're introverts or extroverts, we belong. We are part of a community that contains ourselves, our families and friends, our pets, our neighbors and classmates, people who share our interests, and the people who will eventually fall into our orbit in the future.

ACTIVITY BREAK:
EXPLODING CLASSIFICATIONS

We are so much more than our labels! It can be easy to reduce ourselves down to our stereotypes: the loud one, the funny one, the blonde one. We sort ourselves by *Harry Potter* houses and by our favorite books, movies, television shows, and other fandoms. We may even classify ourselves by our introversion or extroversion. However, we are all complex and so much more than the limitations of classifications.

For example, I am very introverted, but I'm not shy and have a loud voice; most people who don't know me extremely well would believe I'm an extrovert. Despite not being shy, I struggle with social anxiety, likely because my hearing loss makes me self-conscious and concerned about interaction. How are these contradictory things possible? And yet they are.

Take some time to consider and name some of your many labels and classifications, and then explode them. What are your contradictions? In what ways are you more than your labels suggest, or different than you seem? In what ways do you have traits that seem to oppose one another and yet work together to create you? Humans are a rich and contradictory tapestry; as you think, embrace all the clashing colors that compose you.

CHAPTER EIGHT

EFFECTIVE COPING THROUGH GRATITUDE

THE SCIENCE BEHIND GRATITUDE AS HUMAN CONNECTION

The word "gratitude" might remind us of something we get shamed for when we are struggling: *you should be grateful for what you have!* However, this chapter is *not* about the forced positivity of looking on the bright side, counting our blessings, thinking about how "it could be worse," or insisting on being grateful despite our suffering and life obstacles. This chapter is *not* about suggesting we are taking our privileges and people in our lives for granted. In fact, none of these things are helpful to help us grow and cope. When we stigmatize normal emotions like sadness, anger, and fear, we silence our lived experiences and minimize our full range of emotions. We breed shame and encourage each other to bottle up our feelings.

No, this chapter is about ways we can experience true struggles, admit them, *and* see stress benefits from cultivating gratitude.

When we think about gratitude in terms of materialism—what we possess—this can feed back into ineffective thought patterns, guilt, and shame when we compare ourselves to others, looking at the *haves* and *have nots*. Gratitude as comparison is not useful stress relief. It can simply lead to suffering, thinking there's something wrong with us if we "have" so much and still feel so stressed, anxious, or alone. What *is* effective is offering gratitude towards others while allowing ourselves to feel love and appreciation.[1]

Gratitude, at its foundation, is a powerful form of human connection that makes us feel seen and valued. This may seem very sentimental, but when we open ourselves to big feelings of love, loyalty, and gratitude, we open ourselves up to a rich and full life—even if it contains the risk of getting hurt. That risk is worth the reward. Humans are built for social bonds. From infancy, we learn how to communicate by observing the others around us and imitating them experimentally. Eventually, we progress to making real meaning with sounds and gestures. Long before we are old enough to really understand our learned behaviors, our growing brains are already at work collecting responses to our actions and analyzing them. When we get responses we like, we repeat the action. From there, we embark on increasingly complex communication experiments: combining sounds or gestures into words, words into phrases, phrases into sentences. Will we be understood? Will we be seen and wanted?

We've been doing this—making requests for human connection—from birth. From the moment we first cry, we are unconsciously reaching out into the world. When we think about it, every act of human communication began as an experiment in connecting with others, and that connection carries risk. However, the results of successful connection are bigger than the gestures and words we use. Notice how children repeat sounds and gestures over and over again when they like the response they get—a smile, a laugh, a wave. How many of us have had a child wave at us at a store? What happens when we smile and wave back? Receiving nothing more than a "hi" or a wave back can make a child's day. We can see how much humans crave belonging and understanding from a very young age.

Gratitude answers the human call. It is a validation—that what we said or did, in ways big and small, did not go unnoticed. In the world of nearly eight billion people, we were seen. We made a difference. We took our place in the ebb and flow of contact. We were appreciated.

Of course, this chapter is about *giving* gratitude to others, not necessarily *receiving* it back ourselves (although we hope this happens, too).

Interestingly enough, it turns out that giving gratitude does reward us, the givers. Gratitude is one of the most meaningful, and vulnerable, ways of connecting to others. Relentless individualism can be an ineffective shield from the pains of life. In some cases, our independence is a trauma response born from the belief that we can't rely on others who have hurt us. Much like anger is a secondary emotion that can cover more vulnerable feelings beneath, our insistence that we owe nothing to anyone can do the same. Admitting we need someone else, even in the tiniest ways, can feel like a crack in our armor.

However, as much as we might not like it, vulnerability is the price of a full life. As Brené Brown points out, we expose ourselves to our emotions and deepest yearnings for human contact and love when we allow ourselves to be vulnerable: "vulnerability is . . . the cradle of the emotions and experiences that we crave. Vulnerability is the birthplace of love, belonging, joy, courage, empathy, and creativity. It is the source of hope."[2] This is not neediness; we can maintain our independence and still reap stress relief from our bond with others.

The science of gratitude shows that while saying "thank you" might be a fine art and a verbal skill, it is also so much more; in fact, it produces a measurable impact for scientists to quantify and evaluate. Now scientists across a range of disciplines—not only psychology, but also evolutionary biology, genetics, neuroscience, and biomedical science—are testing the ways our minds and bodies feel gratitude. Our language, the words we use that vanish into thin air as we say them, seems so intangible and abstract. Yet new studies show we receive measurable health benefits from telling ourselves and others what we appreciate, and that communication impacts us on a cellular level.

To improve a skill, first we have to successfully identify it. Defining gratitude might be a deceptively simple task. A 2004 study terms gratitude as a twofold state: first is the recognition "that one has obtained a positive outcome," and second is the (often difficult) recognition of having benefitted from "an external source."[3] Offering gratitude isn't just a state of being, but as mentioned before, it is vulnerability. It can

be difficult or even embarrassing to tell someone how they were meaningful to us, how we relied on them or couldn't have done something
without their assistance.

Studies show we reap countless benefits from being grateful. The
Greater Good Science Center at the University of California, Berkeley confirms that gratitude can improve and protect our mental well-
being; openly grateful individuals "report being happier and more satisfied with their lives."[4] Studies suggest individual physical health benefits: "people with higher dispositional gratitude reported better sleep,
less fatigue, and lower levels of cellular inflammation" as well as quicker
illness recovery rates.[5]

How often do we say "thank you"? For most of us, the answer
is probably often! But do we put much thought into the majority of
those times? Sometimes we say "thank you" as empty words so often
it becomes a blur—to the waitstaff at the restaurant when they refill
our water, to the stranger who hands us something we dropped, to
the person who holds the door open for us. And those people deserve
thanks. The person holding the door open has no idea what kind of day
we're having, what mental or emotional burdens we may be carrying;
that door holding might be everything after a long day of catastrophe.

When small gestures like this hold big meaning, we don't *have* to
stop and tell the person it mattered to us (although we can!), but do
take a moment to acknowledge some mental gratitude. Genuine stress
relief benefits come from recognizing that tiny ordinary moments are
the foundations of joy. Life's goodness does not necessarily come from
the big things, but the little gestures and most ordinary times. Practice noticing those small things, from the way a stranger smiles at us
in passing on the street to watching loved ones laugh at their favorite
television show.[6]

It seems so simple a habit to practice, but numerous studies reveal
that doing so offers lowered stress and better mental and physical health
as a result.

BIGGER BENEFITS FROM
ADDING THE PERSONAL

As a stress-relief practice, the words "thank you" don't always seem to say enough or capture quite what we mean! Sometimes it seems like a knee-jerk reaction or a perfunctory saying. How can we truly embrace gratitude for its full health benefits?

This brings us to cake. This isn't about baking cakes to express thanks, although that isn't a bad idea, either. The innovation that inspired the success of the cake mix industry tells us something about how to add value to our gratitude: putting the icing on the cake. Metaphorically, putting the "icing on the cake" means to enhance something, but icing also enhanced the collapsing sales of boxed cake mix in the 1950s.[7] Why? It's not the way mixing butter, sugar, and cream create something delicious, but the *personal touch* of how adding the icing convinces us that we made art. The more of ourselves we put into something—the painstaking effort of design and decoration, spread on with our own hands—the more invested we are. The greater our personal investment, the bigger the psychological benefit. In fact, studies show that giving a full, personalized "gratitude visit" to someone can boost our mental health and physical well-being for *one to three months*.[8]

So how do we personalize our gratitude practices? First, we experiment. Break out of the habit of saying the *same* words to make new brain habits. If we often say "thank you," try "I appreciate you because . . . " Then say, "I love that you . . . " and be specific. That's where the wonderful chemical reaction between words comes in: when we join "thank you" with "because," our meaning changes and becomes more than the sum of its parts. Suddenly, we are being personal, specific, meaningful. Anyone can give thanks, but not just anyone takes the time to say *why* they're thankful. Time and effort matter. When we do so, we also invest ourselves more into the world, and our brains benefit from that engagement.

Most of all, we shouldn't neglect thanking ourselves! Self-appreciation is the first step toward stress relief and healing.

ACTIVITY BREAK: GIVE AND TAKE

Beloved children's television host Mister Rogers said, "All of us, at some time or other, need help. Whether we're giving or receiving help, each one of us has something valuable to bring to this world. That's one of the things that connects us as neighbors—in our own way, each one of us is a giver and a receiver." Note that he points out that we are both—we are not meant to be all givers, nor all receivers.

Take a moment to think about the things tangible and intangible that you have given and received in the last few days or week. Have you given someone a hug? Have you received a text from someone you care about? (Yes! Receiving responses counts—a successful request for connection that receives a response is highly fulfilling.) Have you loaned someone a pen or received some loose-leaf paper when you ran out? Given advice or received suggestions and feedback on something? Consider how you participate in the flow of give and take in the world, and the connections—however momentary, even with strangers—that form.

PART III

ANECDOTES

CHAPTER NINE
PANDEMIC EXPERIENCES

Recent studies on the impact of the COVID-19 pandemic on teenagers revealed that older teenagers ages eighteen to nineteen reported much higher rates of feeling anxious and depressed during the pandemic. This same group also expressed higher percentages of concern about their social anxiety, mental health, and falling behind academically.[1] This is perhaps because this age group stands in transition, on the cusp of new chapters in college, career, and other opportunities that may be more affected by the pandemic.

The following anecdotes come from older teenagers in college reflecting on their pandemic experiences and what they struggled with as a result of their disruptions.

ASHLEY

I was a freshman in college when the COVID-19 pandemic began. I remember hearing the news and thinking it was something that couldn't affect us. Seeing stuff in China and Europe seemed so distant from our lives. In retrospect, that's obviously not true. The world is so connected.

It was a huge disruption to my school and home life—I had to move out of the dorm and back home from my university. I picked a college four and a half hours from home so that I could be independent, and then to feel like it was all being taken away was extremely hard. My best friends live more than eleven hours from my hometown. It'll most likely be four or five months before the next time I can see them, if I *can* even see them.

Back home, school work was more challenging with nowhere quiet to study and so much more being expected from me because I was home to watch my siblings or help around the house on top of my work. It was one thing to help out when I was at home in high school, but some of my classes are really demanding. And I'm a good student, but those classes have been a struggle. I wanted to do so much better my first year of college, but I feel like I didn't learn nearly as much over online courses as I would have in person. I studied strictly for the test rather than for my future.

Ultimately, it's hard to lose almost half of my freshman year. No spring parties, no more time in a college dorm, no first baseball season. So many things that now seem so small, I won't get to experience.

With both parents working from home and my siblings and I all doing school work, we've had both positive *and* negative changes. We have dinner together almost every night, which is nice. But we all fight to find our own space during the day. It seems like the house could never be big enough for us to all have our own space to breathe.

Truthfully, I've noticed I've been more impatient and am quick to become agitated. The lack of friends and the loss of my "normal" life completely threw me off. I've been adjusting to life all over again. Additionally, my grandma contracted COVID and has been dealing with pneumonia most recently. While she is doing well, it reminds us that no family is untouchable. That's scary.

My boyfriend and I have been dating long distance for about two years now, so the idea of being separate may not be new for us, but the amount of time we've had to spend apart is a lot longer than we're used to.

In relation to my friends, I feel as if every one of them has been taken from me and we didn't get to say proper goodbyes. With my roommate, we went from sharing the same room for almost eight months, to a phone call once every week or so.

Going to a university that's almost 60 percent out of state means that my best friends aren't within driving distance to where I live. We thought we were leaving for spring break for two weeks, but ended up being across the country for about seven months. My relationships have gotten me through this, but even my friends in my hometown have been distant because we're all dealing with our own stuff.

BETH

I was in my first year at a university about fourteen hours away from my hometown when the pandemic began. I was aware, but I honestly thought nothing of it. Because I didn't have a TV in my room at school, I didn't watch the news nearly as often. My university is in a bubble, and I didn't really pursue outside of that bubble. I was just looking forward to spring break, part in my hometown, and part in Florida.

Because we got stuck during our spring break, I didn't even move out of the dorm for months and months. Everything shut down the day we drove to Florida. It was happening as we were driving. When we got to the condo that night, we were all trying to cancel flights back to our university and find a way to get home.

For months, I didn't have the majority of my clothes or any of my things in general because they were fourteen hours away in a dorm I couldn't access. The *one* trip where I packed lightly, I wish I didn't. The university shipped us our "necessary" books if we filled out a form telling them where we kept our books in the dorm room. Then, of course, the one time I don't clean my room before break, people need to enter. I feel so bad for those lovely people who packed my things.

The social distancing hurts. My love language is physical touch. And my university is the place where I actually found fruitful friendships. I made time for those friendships for the first time in my life. I've never received so many hugs in my life. I miss all of them. We FaceTime, but I crave that physical affection. No more late-night tacos at 2 a.m. on a Friday. No more playing video games until late night. Ultimately, FaceTime is not quality time for me. It reminds me I can't hug my friends, or take their hand to push through crowds at parties. I miss them dearly.

It's especially hard being away from my boyfriend. He lives about six hours away from me—maybe an easily drivable distance, but because my dad is an essential worker, it's best not to expose my boyfriend's family to anything I might be exposed to. It's heartbreaking because when we said goodbye after spring break, I thought I'd see him soon, and we had plans to go to the beach in a few months. Now it's summer and those plans are canceled. With my family arguing with me all the time, and my friends not around, I really feel alone sometimes.

Living at home again is so *stressful* when I thought I'd sort of left that behind. My classes started giving more work to make sure everyone's doing work and not missing out. Everything was due an hour earlier than usual, even though my day started at the same time.

Then, on top of that, I got all of these family chores. I want to help, but I have a twenty-hour credit workload. I don't have time to do the dishes they wanted me to do at a specific time. I'm working on my future. There was a lot of yelling. My parents didn't understand the amount of work I had, so they thought, *oh, she went off to college and now she's just being selfish*. Their anger wasn't very good for my self-esteem. I just wanted to get back to my old life.

I only get four years of college. Even if that freshman year seemed superficial, it mattered to me. I saw it as a time to bond and make memories we'll talk about for years. I'm pulling out loans now for online education instead of in-person education, and that isn't worth it to me. I worked too hard to get into a good college to go in debt for online school. I'm not getting my student loan value's worth of education, and that's especially depressing.

ALAINA

As someone who scrolls through social media when I get bored, I was aware of COVID-19 when it developed in Wuhan, China. I didn't think it would ever get this serious, and I honestly thought it would never make it over to the United States. Looking back, it was foolish of me to believe it wouldn't become a pandemic. Everything happened so quickly, and before I knew it, life had been drastically changed for everyone.

I watched the news during the whole COVID-19 outbreak and quarantine, but I honestly wish I hadn't. When this mess began, all I saw were negative commentaries about the virus on the news and social media, and it served no benefit to me. I've lessened the amount of time spent listening to the news because it was only sparking anxiety. I started checking this website that lets me see the formation of the curve and the statistics of new cases/deaths. It became reassuring to physically see the curve flattening out and the numbers decreasing over periods of time.

For myself, I've had some emotional setbacks. When this pandemic became serious, it seemed as if a mountain was tumbling down. Having my college courses online was not a walk in the park. I struggled a lot that semester, but I'm proud that I kept going even when I didn't feel like it.

On top of that, I temporarily lost my job at a physical therapy place, which is a second family to me. Not being able to see my coworkers and our patients left me feeling pretty lost. I enjoy doing what I do, and I gain a sense of satisfaction from helping others. In addition to that, I also haven't been able to see my friends or boyfriend in months.

While I am an introverted person, I've felt feelings of sadness and anger regarding not seeing my friends. Even when we're under a stay-at-home order, I've seen people my age choosing to hang out with their friends and significant others anyway. I've been socially distancing because some of my friends are vulnerable or their families are vulnerable. I've been so anxious about infecting other people, since people my age generally do not show symptoms of illness. It has been a frustrating experience watching other people not care.

While my friendships have been fine during this time, my relationship has struggled a bit. I have been with my boyfriend for almost four and a half years, and neither of us have done a long-distance relationship before. I'd say our communication skills are normally great, but during this pandemic, it has declined. Both my boyfriend and I have received a lot more school work since college went remote. When he is

busy, I am not. When I am busy, he is not. It almost feels like we are two
ships in the night at times. However, we have discussed these issues and
have been trying to work it out. I'm not sure we'll make it. We're trying.
We're both worried about our academics and the health of our families.

In all honesty, I feel like I learned nothing when school went
online during the second half of the semester. My professors were
very unorganized and threw assignments at us left and right. I have
pretty much had to teach myself my material, which has been no easy
feat—especially physics. I've had several doubts about my academics
because I am trying to graduate a semester early. Because of this, I
have also had concerns about applying to physical therapy programs
because my GRE score is not as high as it needs to be, and I am unable
to retake it due to testing center closures. But, I am doing the best I
can do and that is all that matters!

In the end, I do feel like I missed out on a lot. I missed being at work,
being at school, hanging out with my friends, and going to the gym.
While there was nothing I could really do to fix the absence of work and
school in my life for long stretches of time, FaceTime has been helpful.

To cope with missing the gym, I have been running a lot more. It
has been nice to have that method of stress relief still.

CHAPTER TEN

DISASTER EXPERIENCES

In the face of climate change, catastrophic natural disasters are becoming an increasingly common occurrence marking the lives of adolescents around the globe. The following anecdotes come from adolescents reflecting on their recent experiences with Hurricane Ida in October 2021, and what they struggled with as a result.

ANASTASIA

My dad is not a great person to be stuck in a house with. He has a bad temper, and he only cares about himself, basically.

So, Hurricane Ida knocked out the entire city's electricity, and it was going to be maybe a couple weeks before we had power. Everyone in the house was already stressed out. Like, that makes sense. Who wouldn't be? It's hot. Not a little hot, really hot. We're trying to conserve bottled water and canned goods because we don't know exactly how long we won't have power and how long stores and everything will be closed.

But my dad always takes his stress out on everyone else. I hate him. Can I say that? I do.

Anyway, we were lucky enough to have a small generator. It wasn't big enough to power the whole house or any appliances, but we were using it to charge our cell phones and run a floor fan to cool us off. My dad is a big guy, so out of everyone, he was probably the one feeling the heat and sweating the most.

There was nothing to do without electricity, so I walked around the neighborhood a little just to get out of the house and check on the damage on the other streets. When I got back home, I realized I was pretty overheated and starting to feel a little bit sick. I forgot that when I got home, I wasn't going to go inside with the normal air conditioning on and that it would be hot and stuffy inside, too. I'm dripping sweat and red in the face. Probably going to pass out. But then I remembered we had the fan.

The floor fan wasn't huge, but it was definitely big enough for two people. Me sitting by the fan wasn't going to steal away all the cool air from my dad. He was sitting in front of it, and I didn't think there would be a problem if I sat there for a little bit too. However, my dad pretty much lost his mind and started screaming at me. He told me that I was a selfish, spoiled child. According to him, sitting by the fan when I was feeling sick meant I was trying to take something I didn't need.

It's one of those things that's always happening. He's always exploding about nothing and making everyone walk on eggshells. But things like the pandemic or a hurricane make it ten times worse. He's exhausting and honestly, he can be really scary. Then he wonders why we don't have a better relationship. It's because I live walking on eggshells around him.

LINDSEY

Leaving my pets behind was terrifying. I was so upset. We evacuated for Hurricane Ida because my mom had been in the hospital with COVID, and I think she had only gotten out a week or two before. She was too weak to deal with the stress of getting ready to shelter through the storm. Hurricane preparation is a lot, and my dad was working. Plus, dealing with the heat was going to be really unhealthy for her recovery if we lost power for a while. I understood why we had to leave, but I was stressed and pretty mad at my parents because we had to leave our two cats.

Our cats hate getting in the car and can't deal with car rides because they think they're going to the vet. My dad said there was only so much room in the car for the three of us and our stuff, it was hard to find a hotel room that would allow pets, and we were going to be on the road for hours. We left them lots of food and water, but pretty much all I could think about was how scared my poor pets were going to be all alone through the storm.

It's not like we planned a vacation where we could get someone to watch them or board them somewhere. My grandpa said he would check on them, but if there was a lot of damage the roads were going to be closed. I just wanted them to be with us.

The trip was supposed to be about five hours to get to our hotel out of state, but it ended up taking us twelve or thirteen hours because of the traffic since everyone was on the road evacuating, too. I know that the cats would have been miserable stuck in their carriers the whole time.

But I missed them and was scared that something would happen to them since they were going to be alone for days. I was worried about getting home to my cats pretty much the *whole* time we were out of state. I cried every time I thought about them. That's not even embarrassing, they're my best friends.

When we got back, they seemed mostly okay, though the one that gets nervous was hiding in the garage a lot. I feel pretty guilty about abandoning them.

ABBY

I think the hardest, most stressful part about the hurricane was the waiting and not knowing how everyone was doing.

All my friends whose houses weren't too badly damaged were saying the most stressful part was how hot it was without air conditioning. And some of my friends and family had a lot of damage—like, they can't stay in their house because the roof is so messed up or a tree fell on their house. Our house needs some roof repairs but we're mostly okay, so I think for me it wasn't just that no one had any power and we were hot and thirsty and bored, but we didn't have almost any cell phone reception for a couple days. I don't mean that just like, "Oh, I can't get on TikTok," but not being able to talk with people like normal was really hard.

When the storm started, I was a little nervous but felt mostly okay. I knew my mom would have made us leave if she thought we would be in real danger. Before it got dark, I was texting my friends and my cousins and stuff while the storm was starting. We were talking about how the wind was picking up, how we started seeing things flying by from the window, and then how we were hearing things crashing into each other. Or like, how loud the sound of power transformers exploding is, which I didn't know until I heard it. Texting kind of made it a little less scary because it was like we were just having conversation. We would be like, "Oh, the power just blinked but it came back on! We still have power!"

But then the power and internet finally went out. Around the same time that happened, it started where no one could send messages or get on any of the apps. My mom and my brother were walking around the house holding their phones high and low, trying to get service bars, looking everywhere to see if regular service or data would kick in.

Once the sun set, all you could do was sit around and listen to these terrible noises without being able to see what was happening. No streetlights or any other lights were on outside, so it's really, really pitch black. My brother was stupid enough to open the front door for a second to see if he could see outside, but at least he realized pretty quick that he couldn't see a thing and was going to get hurt.

My mom started getting pretty worked up about losing cell service because it reminded her of Hurricane Katrina. I wasn't born yet, but she said their phones pretty much didn't work for weeks and weeks afterward.

Once I realized that none of us could call for help or let anyone know if there was a problem, I got really stressed. Then I just sat in the dark and listened to the wind and all the crashes and banging and thought about how bad the wind sounded. My phone didn't distract me anymore. I could definitely hear trees falling and things crashing and breaking, so not being able to talk to my friends about if they were okay was hard.

It ended up being only a couple days that we really couldn't use our phones, though they were kind of glitchy and had a lot of delays for a little longer than that. The hurricane made me realize how much I use my phone as a distraction when I'm stressed, though.

LIZZIE

I'm not saying I always understood this because I didn't, but the most stressful part is that hurricanes aren't over when the storm is over. Not everyone has insurance or can afford to fix what they lost, you know? And even if you do have insurance, there's still deductibles you have to pay that are pretty huge. Not everything you lose can be replaced. Our apartment roof pretty much came off, and we lost a ton of things inside our apartment to water damage that I'll never be able to get back. We had renter's insurance on the apartment, but there's this huge deductible, and I know we really don't have it. Whatever check we end up getting to cover what we lost really isn't going to cover it.

It's not just that a lot of our clothes and furniture are messed up. I'm not trying to be all materialistic.

There are pictures of me with my grandparents who died, my Maw Maw and Paw Paw, that got ruined. I think I cried the most over those pictures because we don't have the original files for them anymore. I can't just print new ones. A bunch of my dance team ribbons and pictures and awards got ruined, too. My little sister had to throw some of her art projects away, and it's heartbreaking to see a crying eight-year-old who was really proud of what she made, you know?

Some of my mom's scrapbooks got ruined. There's a lot of stuff you don't realize you can't just replace if they get wet and covered in mold. Those are lost memories forever.

PART IV

ADDITIONAL STRATEGIES AND RESOURCES

CHAPTER ELEVEN

COPING STRATEGIES:
THOUGHTS

UNDERSTANDING THE AMYGDALA HIJACK

When we're in distress, it can be difficult to think clearly.
There is a neurological reason for that: it's because the part of the brain that controls automatic behavior like detecting threats and triggering the stress response (the amygdala) works faster than the part of the brain that controls conscious decision-making (the frontal lobes). It takes the amygdala about one-fiftieth of a second (yes, a mere fraction of a single second!) to activate a stress response, versus the frontal lobe's comparatively slow three seconds for its decision-making. In terms of survival, this is a good thing. If we took three seconds to decide consciously to step out of the way of a speeding car, we'd get smashed flat.

However, the downside to this is that once the amygdala has triggered our stress hormones, it prevents our frontal lobes from coming online and effectively "hijacks" control from the rational, conscious part of our brain.[1] Our anxious thoughts are already off and running before we're even consciously aware of a problem.

How can we avoid giving in to irrational behavior guided by stress hormones that urge us to fight or flee when those aren't effective choices? How can we stop and think clearly and logically when our logic brain has been shut down, *literally*?

We've already completed the first step! One of the best ways to take control of our amygdala's responses is to understand how those responses work and begin thinking about what is and isn't a threat to us while we're in calm moments. With time and practice, we can train our amygdalas to stop issuing stress hormones over certain triggers when we understand what they're doing and why. When we understand how the stress response functions, the stressors that set us off, and are able to consider why they may not be as concerning as our amygdala initially wants us to think they are, our brain is less likely to flag them as a threat next time they arise.

When we recognize the fight-or-flight response for what it is, take note of the stressors and emotions that brought us to that moment. That brief beat of recognition may slow us long enough to hit the "stop" button on the amygdala's high alert and bring back our conscious frontal lobe functioning. It's okay if we aren't able to recognize what's happening in the moment until after it's over; that's what the amygdala hijack does once the stress hormone train starts rolling. Still, pause after the fight-or-flight moment to review what sparked it, the thoughts and emotions that occurred during it, and the behaviors with which we responded. That recognition can help keep the amygdala calm for next time. Basically, we need our amygdalas to say, "I recognize this as a potential trigger from last time, but it's just a moment of high emotion, not a life-or-death threat," and to not issue the hormonal alarm. There is always next time!

OBSERVING THOUGHTS

This book suggests numerous times to pause before acting in order to observe our thoughts and emotions. This is training to stop the amygdala hijack.

It's also training for *habit*. Human minds are prone to falling into ineffective thinking habits when we are strained under too much stress or experiencing anxiety. When we pay attention to our own thinking processes before acting, however, we can notice when our thoughts are leading us astray. Thoughts are not always rational! Common "thinking errors"—the ways our minds assume, distort, or exaggerate what we perceive—include blaming ourselves for situations, expecting experiences to turn out as worst-case scenarios, or overgeneralizing.

Before we fall into a self-blame trap for how we think, remember that thought patterns aren't *us*; they're just thoughts—invisible, intangible, and we can let them drift off without acting on them at all. Also, those thoughts are simply a product of our habits, and habits can be changed. We are not alone in making some thinking errors. These are habits we have picked up from our home environments, have witnessed in others around us daily, and in many cases have been pushed into due to trauma or anxiety.

The human brain is always learning. It is not set into a permanent shape, and we can build new neural pathways to improve our thought habits with practice. New habits can be formed at any point, at any age, although adolescence is the best time to build those habits and wire them into our brains for a lifetime.

BLACK-AND-WHITE THINKING

This is sometimes referred to as all-or-nothing thinking. When we think in black and white, we see only the either/or possibilities; we don't allow room for the neutral, gray, or middle-ground possibilities. Most things in life aren't either/or, yes/no, everything/nothing propositions, but allow for a complex range of nuances. Examples of black-and-white thinking include:

- I got a C on this test, so I'm bad at math.

- I didn't get on the team, so it's not worth trying out for something else.

- If I can't get into my dream college, I'm a failure.

- I'm not talented at clarinet if I don't make first chair in band.

BLAME-TAKING

When we personalize our experiences as our fault, including things that aren't our responsibility or were only partially our responsibility, this is blame-taking. But taking blame and taking responsibility are two different things. We can take responsibility for what we didn't do (like admitting, "I should have paid more attention because I mistakenly read the wrong chapter in the book") without taking blame ("it's my fault the class discussion didn't go well").

Examples of blame-taking include:

- My parents are divorcing because raising me put a burden on their relationship.

- The group project went poorly because I couldn't get myself organized.

- My significant other is unhappy today, so I must have done something to set them off.

- My friend can't meet me after school today because she has work, so she's probably avoiding me.

EMOTIONAL REASONING

Emotional reasoning assumes that our feelings are accurate and based in evidence when they are not. Feelings aren't facts—they can be misplaced, arise from misconceptions, or emerge out of habit. Examples of emotional reasoning include:

- I feel anxious in the cafeteria, so people must be looking at me and laughing.

- I feel sad because of a breakup, so everyone knows I'm unloved and a loser.

- I feel overwhelmed today, so I'm failing to cope with my responsibilities, and my family is disappointed in me.

LABELING

Human minds like categorizing things, so we often tell ourselves negative stories or make unhealthy labels for ourselves and the others in our lives. We can stick too strongly to these labels, reducing ourselves and others down to stereotypes or single "types," accepting them as factual reality. Examples of labeling include:

- I'm too sensitive and shy.

- She's not smart.

- He's just a jock.

OVERGENERALIZING

When we overgeneralize, we take one negative experience and use it to describe all others, regardless of the differences. We draw much broader conclusions about an experience based on very limited evidence, believing that something that happened once sets how it will always be. Overgeneralizing tends to lean on "absolute" words like *every, always,* and *never.* Examples of overgeneralizing include:

- People never pick me for their groups or teams.

- I missed that last goal, so I suck at soccer.

- I couldn't trust a friend or family member, so there's no point in making other connections or relationships.

- Someone hurt me, so I won't date again because love is always cruel.

WORST-CASE-SCENARIO THINKING

Sometimes referred to as catastrophizing. Negative *what ifs* plague this thinking habit. This thought pattern occurs when we let the domino cascade of possibilities carry us away (. . . and then if this happens, then . . .) into imagining how something will affect us in the worst possible way.

The tantalizing nature of this line of thinking is that these bad scenarios *could* theoretically happen. However, in this case, we take minor issues and blow them up into something bigger than we can cope with beforehand, and we don't take into account the *unlikelihood* of these worst imaginings coming true. "We'll deal with that possibility *if* it occurs" is a good counter to any worst-case thoughts you may have. Examples of worst-case-scenario thinking include:

- If I don't get an A in physical science then I can't take AP Biology, and then I won't get into a good college, so I'll never become a veterinarian.

- If I go to the dance alone, everyone will know I didn't go with anybody, then no one will ask me out to future dances. I'll be doomed to unpopularity and die alone.

WAYS TO EXAMINE AND ADJUST THINKING ERRORS

PUTTING THOUGHTS IN REVIEW

When we look at thoughts that get us upset or leave us feeling unsettled and stressed, we can weigh them first before making any decisions or actions. Much like a pros/cons chart, we can list the evidence in our head for/against those thoughts being reasonable concerns.

While it might help to literally draw out a chart, we can do this mentally as well. What evidence do we have for this thought? Evidence should be factual—not opinion, emotion, or things we have heard as possibility. We can place our anxious thoughts in review to list why we believe our thoughts are a realistic possibility and why they might not be something to seriously internalize.

ANXIOUS
THOUGHTS IN REVIEW

REALISTIC?

Nervous about wisdom teeth removal surgery.

-Getting my wisdom teeth removed might be painful.
-There will be swelling and it'll be hard to eat other than soft food.
-It might be a couple of weeks before everything is healed.
-Any surgery and anesthetic has risk. However, I can talk to the oral surgeon about the risks and anesthesia used and make sure I feel comfortable.

UNREALISTIC?

Don't get the surgery because something could happen like a reaction to anesthesia, damage my gums or teeth, etc.

-Not getting it done will mess up my other teeth because my jaw isn't big enough.
-Mom and Dad both had theirs removed without problems. I think Sam did, too. Can ask.
-The surgeon has been practicing fifteen years. Has good online reviews.

Our thoughts can overwhelm us and mislead us into additional stress and anxiety. Making evidence tables (either weighing the evidence in our heads or filling out a chart like this) can help us weigh our thoughts as realistic or recognize them as anxious thinking errors. Download a free blank version from the author's website at christiecognevich.com. *Illustration by Christie Cognevich.*

CONSIDERING ALTERNATE OUTCOMES

What if things went *right*? What if things went just *okay*? Even if the worst did happen, would it be as disastrous as we worry it could be? Consider the thought and the negative outcome we're concerned about. What are some other possible, different outcomes? When we can think flexibly—seeing alternatives as simply *different* and not the *worst*, and even allowing ourselves to accept that the best could happen—we break out of negative thinking patterns that make us stress more than necessary. It can help to write out a list to see just how many ways something can turn out well or acceptably well.

RELEASING EXPECTATIONS

Multitasking is exhausting. Having expectations of ourselves can be perfectly healthy and effective, but sometimes we put entirely too much pressure on ourselves to perform perfectly or do it all.

It can be difficult to recognize and give ourselves credit for what we *do* get done in a day. Even harder for some is practicing letting go of one expectation per day without beating ourselves up mentally. While that expectation shouldn't be something major, nor should we let go of the same expectation day after day so it never gets done—it would not be effective to drop the expectation of going to school every day—when we give ourselves permission to drop one demand, we give ourselves breathing room.

Being healthier about our priorities means letting ourselves rearrange and drop things here and there as needed. Nothing terrible will happen if one time, we skip a nightly instrument practice in favor of getting some much-needed sleep. Very little will be missed if we don't scroll through our social media feed or respond to those non-urgent emails until the morning. And if the difference between an A+ essay and just a regular A is going to cost us an hour or two of agonizing perfectionism, perhaps it's best to move on to the next assignment.

When we become more agile at weighing the mental cost versus the benefit, we can quiet our inner voice telling us we're not doing enough.

FOCUS THOUGHTS ON WHAT WE CAN CONTROL

It can be a frustrating fact of life that the things that matter to us aren't always the things we can control. There are some things we simply won't be able to change, ever. Getting stuck in a weary thought loop of *if only* is miserable and self-defeating.

We cannot change the families we were born to, but we can build chosen families out of friends. We cannot change whether someone agrees to go out with us or not, but we can control how we respond to rejection in an appropriate way. We cannot change yesterday, but we can control how we tackle now and tomorrow.

There's a difference between acceptance of what we can't control ("I won't waste my thoughts fighting a brick wall") and self-defeat or helplessness ("there's nothing I can do about it, so I'm stuck").

CHAPTER TWELVE

COPING STRATEGIES: EMOTIONS

EMOTIONAL SELF-REFLECTION THROUGH JOURNALING

We mentioned already that journaling can be an excellent strategy for stress management. In many cases, it can be an outlet for our most intense or troubling emotions when we take them out of our bodies and place them on the page instead.

- Fear. What were you afraid of when you were younger that you aren't afraid of anymore—like sleeping alone or with the lights off? Is there anything you weren't afraid of as a child that you're no longer willing to do—like sing or dance in public?

- Sadness. What was the last thing you felt sad about? Was it profound sadness or a minor disappointment? How do you tell the difference between the depths of your sadness—how do various kinds of sad moments feel different for you?

- Anger. What sort of things make us feel mild irritation? What sort of things make us truly angry? Are there certain people we get the angriest with, and why? (Is it because we care about them—what they say, do, and believe—the most?) What is it that they do to get under our skin, and what can we do to improve that? What can we communicate to them that might improve our healthy interactions with less anger?

- Joy. Recall a time when we laughed incredibly hard and couldn't stop—what sparked that, and what was so funny/good about that moment? What are our top joyful childhood moments, and why? What was our most joyful moment in the last year or two, and why? What did that joy feel like, physically? Where did we feel it in our bodies?

EMOTIONAL SKETCHES

Sometimes we feel more comfortable doodling than writing out our emotions. Keeping an art journal or simply drawing on scratch paper is just as useful an emotional outlet. None of these have to be literally interpreted—you can doodle metaphors or abstract ideas. If you're not artistically inclined, don't be afraid to use stick figures and other little doodles; no one is judging.

- What are three emotions you've experienced in the last day? Doodle what they look like inside you.

- When was the last time you felt excited about a possibility? Doodle what your body looks like inside when it's filled with anticipation.

- Think of the last time someone did a kind gesture for you. How did you feel before and then after? Doodle a before-and-after comparison of your emotional states.

- Close your eyes and imagine a moment of joy (either a real memory or an ideal version). What does it look like? Doodle it out.

- Yesterday my (insert emotion here) looked like . . . / Today my (insert emotion here) looked like . . . / Tomorrow I hope/think my (insert emotion here) will look like . . .

- The inside of my brain when I'm (insert emotion here) looks like . . . / The inside of my brain when (insert emotion here) passes looks like . . .

- Doodle what you look like when you feel happiest in your skin. What sort of things surround you?

CHAPTER THIRTEEN

COPING STRATEGIES: BODY

Taking care of our bodies is one of the most controllable aspects of stress. While we can't always anticipate or avoid stressors, we can typically provide our body with what it needs to stay healthier, more nourished, and therefore more likely to be calmer and in less distress.

It may seem obvious, but sometimes we can neglect our most simple needs without realizing that basics like sleep, hydration, nutrition, and active movement are the foundation for the rest of our mental, emotional, and physical well-being.

The following are all small, low-impact ways to take care of our bodies. They are deliberately gentle and fairly easy suggestions. For mobility problems, sensory sensitivity, and other personal issues, we can always skip suggestions that don't work for our needs. And remember—we don't always listen to our body when it asks for more or less socialization, sensory input, movement, sleep, hydration, and nutrition, but we can practice doing so and get better at recognizing our needs.

AWARENESS OF OUR PHYSICAL SIGNS

Everyone reacts to stress differently. We covered the common physical symptoms of stress in chapter 1, but sometimes we forget to pay attention to where we feel stress or anxiety in tense moments. Additionally, pay attention to any nervous physical habits we might have such as playing with our hair, tapping our feet or fingers, jiggling our leg, or biting our nails. We are not always conscious of when we're under stress, and we can prepare ourselves to react better if we can read the signs beforehand.

SUGGESTIONS FOR PHYSICAL SELF-CARE

These can be done any day, at any time. Some of these are excellent suggestions for relaxation in particularly stressful moments.

- Play with your pets

- Go for a walk—whether by yourself, or with a friend or family member, or your pets.

- Hug someone, or if you're not comfortable with human touch (for whatever reason!), hug a pet or a pillow, or even yourself.

- Do some stretches and gentle movement for a few minutes—it doesn't have to be a full exercise routine, but get up and move around a little.

- Go outside and touch something for a few minutes—take off your shoes and feel the dirt or grass with your toes, or the light on your skin.

- Take a long shower or bath.

- Clean your room or organize a drawer.

- Go swimming.

- Take a few slow, deep breaths every so often.

- Watch a cooking show or video with a friend or family member, then try to replicate it together (or do this alone!).

- Flip through an old photo album with an older family member and listen to their stories.

- Experiment with water—drink it at room temperature and then ice-cold, and figure out what you like better, or try some unsweetened flavored water or flavor drops.

PRACTICING BETTER "SLEEP HYGIENE"

As our bodies and brains are growing, one of the most essential foundational needs we can take care of is getting good rest. Without enough sleep, our mental and emotional states become highly disrupted along with our physical health. "Sleep hygiene" is a strategy that helps us maintain regular good sleep.

- Go to bed and wake up at a consistent time every day, even on weekends.

- Get a full eight to ten hours of sleep per night. Yes, that many— teenagers need more sleep as they grow!

- Avoid substances that can disrupt sleep or affect sleep quality, including caffeine, nicotine, and alcohol.

- Use the bed for sleep only! We can train our bodies to associate the bed with bedtime; getting in bed triggers sleepiness. Avoid doing work, watching television, using the laptop, or reading in bed; do them elsewhere and move to the bed only when done.

- Don't use screens at least an hour before bedtime to avoid light disruption. Use nighttime or dark mode settings on apps after the sun goes down.

CHAPTER FOURTEEN

QUICK GUIDE TO RESOURCES

Some of the information below is printed elsewhere in this book, but for ease of access, these mental health resources are listed here as well.

Remember, if you or a loved one are facing a mental health emergency, including thinking about suicide or self-harm, call one of the help lines listed below or go to the emergency room immediately.

Even if you feel hopeless to act or don't know what to do to help your stress, others can help. Pause, breathe, then reach out to one of the resources listed here as soon as possible. There are many safe, confidential, free, immediate options available for you to talk, text, or chat online with someone if you are in crisis.

These services are designed to provide people to talk and stay with you until you have moved out of extreme distress into a calmer mindset. You never have to experience crisis alone.

You do not need to hesitate or ask yourself if your issues are serious enough to contact any of these numbers. These options are available for *anyone* who needs to talk about *any* issue, regardless of the "seriousness" of your problems or mental health.

MENTAL HEALTH RESOURCES

United States:

- Call 911 for an emergency, or the 24/7 National Suicide Prevention Hotline at 1-800-273-8255. There are options for Spanish speakers and the deaf/hard of hearing.

- If you feel more comfortable texting, the Crisis Text Line (https:// www.crisistextline.org/) is a free text message service available for people in crisis, available 24/7 in English or Spanish. Text HOME to 741741. It is available on WhatsApp and Facebook Messenger, as well.

- The National Alliance on Mental Illness (NAMI) HelpLine (nami. org) can be reached Monday through Friday, 10 a.m. to 10 p.m. EST at 1-800-950-NAMI or via email at info@nami.org.

- If you feel more comfortable texting, NAMI has a free text message service for people in crisis, available 24/7. Text NAMI to 741741.

- NAMI also has an online chat feature available on its website.

Canada:

- Call 911 for an emergency, or the 24/7 Kids Help phone service (anyone under the age of twenty) at 1-800-668-6868 or Crisis Services Canada (no age restriction) at 1-833-456-4566. Quebec residents can call Crisis Services at 1-866-277-3553.

- If you feel more comfortable texting, the Crisis Text Line (https:// www.crisistextline.ca/) is a free text message service for people in crisis, available 24/7 in English or French. Text HOME (in English) or PARLER (in French) to 686868.

United Kingdom:

- Call 999 for an emergency, or the National Health Service's First Response Service for mental health at 111, Option 2.

- If you feel more comfortable texting, Shout (https://giveusashout .org/) is a free text message service for people in crisis, available 24/7. Text SHOUT to 85258.

Ireland:

- Call 112 for an emergency, or the Samaritans emotional support helpline at 116 123.

- If you feel more comfortable texting, the Crisis Text Line (https://text50808.ie/) is a free text message service for people in crisis, available 24/7. Text HELLO to 50808.

Australia:

- Call 000 for an emergency, or the 24/7 Kids Helpline phone service (anyone under the age of twenty-five) at 1800 55 1800, or Lifeline (no age restriction) at 13 11 14.

- Both Lifeline (https://www.lifeline.org.au/) and Kids Helpline (https://www.kidshelpline.com.au/) have online chat features available on their respective websites.

- If you feel more comfortable texting, the Lifeline Text is available from 12 p.m. to 6 a.m. AEDT at 0477 13 11 14.

ABUSIVE RELATIONSHIP RESOURCES

If you are experiencing abuse, aren't sure if what you're experiencing is abuse, or have questions or concerns about your relationships, there are resources and advocates out there for you.

Do you have questions or need to check in with someone? Do you need help? There are many safe, confidential, free, immediate options available for you to talk, text, or chat with someone if you are concerned, confused, have questions, or need to talk about your relationship dynamics.

United States:

- Call loveisrespect (https://www.loveisrespect.org/) at 1-866-331-9474. There are options for Spanish speakers and the deaf/hard of hearing. There is also a live online chat available with advocates on the website.

- If you feel more comfortable texting, text LOVEIS to 22522.

Canada:

- There are a range of options available for you depending on your province. The Ending Violence Association of Canada has a list available on its website at http://endingviolencecanada.org/getting-help/.

United Kingdom:

- Call the National Domestic Abuse Helpline (https://www.national dahelpline.org.uk/) at 0808 2000 247.

Ireland:

- Call the Women's Aid 24-hour National Freephone Helpline (https://www.womensaid.ie/services/helpline.html) at 1800 341 900.

Australia:

- Call 1800RESPECT at 1800 737 732. There is also an online chat service on the website (https://www.1800respect.org.au/).

ADDITIONAL RESOURCES

- The National Alliance on Mental Illness (https://www.nami.org/) provides helpful insights and resources to support individuals with mental illness. It has local chapters throughout the United States.

- The Ok2Talk website (https://ok2talk.org/) is a safe space for you to post and read about what others are experiencing.

FOR LGBTQ+ INDIVIDUALS

- The Trevor Project (https://www.thetrevorproject.org/) provides a supportive, judgment-free community specifically for LGBTQ teens. It offers crisis intervention and suicide prevention services for people under age twenty-five.

- The LGBT National Hotline (https://www.glbthotline.org/) has a dedicated youth hotline for the LGBTQ and questioning community ages twenty-five and younger at 800-246-7743, available Monday through Friday from 4 p.m. to midnight EST and Saturday from noon to 5 p.m. EST.

- The Trans Lifeline (https://translifeline.org/) offers supportive emotional and financial resources for trans individuals in crisis. It provides a hotline at 1-877-565-8860 (United States) and 1-877-330-6366 (Canada).

FOR BIPOC INDIVIDUALS

- The BlackLine (https://www.callblackline.com/) provides safe, judgment-free crisis counseling and social justice resources for black, indigenous, and people of color in the United States. Additionally, BlackLine provides safe avenues for sharing racial injustice.

- Therapy for Black Girls (https://therapyforblackgirls.com/) provides resources for promoting mental health in black girls and women.

- SanaMente (https://www.sanamente.org/) provides mental health resources in Spanish that are culturally focused on the Latinx community.

- The Asian Mental Health Collective (https://www.asianmhc.org/) provides mental health resources that are culturally focused on the Asian community worldwide.

- We R Native (https://www.wernative.org/) provides cultural support and general wellness resources created by indigenous youth for indigenous youth.

NOTES

AUTHOR NOTE

1. Mary Helen Immordino-Yang, Joanna A. Christodoulou, and Vanessa Singh, "Rest Is Not Idleness: Implications of the Brain's Default Mode for Human Development and Education," *Perspectives on Psychological Science* 7, no. 4 (July 2012): 352–64, https://doi .org/10.1177/1745691612447308.

INTRODUCTION: STRESS AND THE PROBLEM WITH TIME

1. Amol Rajan, "OED Word of the Year Expanded for 'Unprecedented' 2020," *BBC News*, November 23, 2020, https://www.bbc.com/news /entertainment-arts-55016543.
2. Associated Press, "Study: 'Time' Is Most Often Used Noun," *CBS News*, June 22, 2006, https://www.cbsnews.com/news/study-time-is-most-of ten-used-noun/.

CHAPTER 1. EXPLORING STRESS

1. Nancy A. Piotrowski and David Wason Hollar, Jr., "Stress," *Magill's Medical Guide Online Edition* (Pasadena, CA: Salem Press, 2019), http:// search.ebscohost.com/login.aspx?direct=true&db=ers&AN=89093 561&site=eds-live&scope=site.
2. Nada Krapić, Jasna Hudek-Knezevic, and Igor Kardum, "Stress in Adolescence: Effects on Development," *International Encyclopedia of the*

Social & Behavioral Sciences (Amsterdam: Elsevier, 2015), https://doi
.org/10.1016/B978-0-08-097086-8.23031-6, 562.

3. Peter Jaret, "The Surprising Benefits of Stress," The Greater Good
   Science Center at the University of California Berkeley, October 20,
   2015, https://greatergood.berkeley.edu/article/item/the_surprising
   _benefits_of_stress.

4. Piotrowski and Hollar, Jr., "Stress."

5. Virginia L. Goetsch and Kevin T. Larkin, "Physiological Responses
   to Stress," *Salem Press Encyclopedia of Health* (Pasadena, CA: Salem
   Press, 2019), http://search.ebscohost.com/login.aspx?direct=true&db
   =ers&AN=93872155&site=eds-live&scope=site.

6. Edward A. Charlesworth and Ronald G. Nathan, *Stress Management:
   A Comprehensive Guide to Wellness* (New York: Ballantine Books,
   2004), 29.

7. Center for Adolescent Health, "Teen Stress," Johns Hopkins Bloomberg
   School of Public Health, 2009, https://www.jhsph.edu/research/cen
   ters-and-institutes/center-for-adolescent-health/_docs/policy-briefs
   /mental-health/teen_stress.pdf.

8. Goetsch and Larkin, "Physiological Responses to Stress."

9. Shelley E. Taylor, "Tend and Befriend Theory," in Paul A. M. Van
   Lange, Arie W. Kruglanski, and E. Tory Higgins (eds.), *The Handbook
   of Theories of Social Psychology* (London: Sage Publications, 2012), 32.

10. Taylor, "Tend and Befriend Theory," 37.

11. Taylor, "Tend and Befriend Theory," 41.

12. Scott Zimmer, "Oxytocin," *Salem Press Encyclopedia of Health* (Pasa-
    dena, CA: Salem Press, 2020), http://search.ebscohost.com/login.aspx
    ?direct=true&db=ers&AN=87324180&site=eds-live&scope=site.

13. Gayle L. Brosnan-Watters, "Fight-or-Flight Response," *Salem Press Ency-
    clopedia of Health* (Pasadena, CA: Salem Press, 2019), http://search.eb
    scohost.com/login.aspx?direct=true&db=ers&AN=93871966&site=
    eds-live&scope=site.

14. Jaret, "The Surprising Benefits of Stress."

15. Brosnan-Watters, "Fight-or-Flight Response."

16. Goetsch and Larkin, "Physiological Responses to Stress."

Chapter 2. Experiencing Long-Term Stress in a Chaotic World

1. Katherine Schaeffer, "Most U.S. Teens Who Use Cellphones Do It to Pass Time, Connect with Others, Learn New Things," Pew Research Center, August 23, 2019, https://www.pewresearch.org/fact-tank/2019/08/23/most-u-s-teens-who-use-cellphones-do-it-to-pass-time-connect-with-others-learn-new-things/.

2. Susan David, *Emotional Agility: Get Unstuck, Embrace Change, and Thrive in Work and Life* (New York: Penguin Random House, 2016), 218.

3. Nancy A. Piotrowski and David Wason Hollar, Jr., "Stress," *Magill's Medical Guide Online Edition* (Pasadena, CA: Salem Press, 2019), http://search.ebscohost.com/login.aspx?direct=true&db=ers&AN=89093561&site=eds-live&scope=site.

4. Brené Brown, *Daring Greatly: How the Courage to Be Vulnerable Transforms the Way We Live, Love, Parent, and Lead* (New York: Penguin Random House, 2012), 22.

5. Brown, *Daring Greatly*, 23.

6. Brown, *Daring Greatly*, 25.

7. Brown, *Daring Greatly*, 27.

8. Drew DeSilver, "The Concerns and Challenges of Being a U.S. Teen: What the Data Show," Pew Research Center, February 26, 2019, https://www.pewresearch.org/fact-tank/2019/02/26/the-concerns-and-challenges-of-being-a-u-s-teen-what-the-data-show/.

9. "Prevalence of Any Anxiety Disorder among Adolescents," National Institute of Mental Health, https://www.nimh.nih.gov/health/statistics/any-anxiety-disorder#part_2578 (accessed October 4, 2021).

10. "CovEx Results," Centers for Disease Control and Prevention, last reviewed March 18, 2021, https://www.cdc.gov/healthyyouth/data/covex/Covex_results.htm.

11. Kelsey Osgood, Hannah Sheldon-Dean, and Henry Kimball, "2021 Children's Mental Health Report," Child Mind Institute, 2021, https://childmind.org/wp-content/uploads/2021/10/CMHR-2021-FINAL.pdf, 11.

12. "A Return to 'Normal': Assessing Mental Health Concerns Among U.S. Teens," Morgan Stanley Alliance for Children's Mental Health, August 2021, https://www.morganstanley.com/assets/pdfs/reemer gence-program-teen-survey-factsheet.pdf, 1.

13. "A Return to 'Normal,'" 3.

14. Osgood et al., "2021 Children's Mental Health Report," 6.

15. "A Return to 'Normal,'" 7.

16. Gayle L. Brosnan-Watters, "Fight-or-Flight Response," *Salem Press Encyclopedia of Health* (Pasadena, CA: Salem Press, 2019), http://search.ebscohost.com/login.aspx?direct=true&db=ers&AN =93871966&site=eds-live&scope=site.

17. Piotrowski and Hollar, Jr., "Stress."

18. Nadine Burke Harris, *The Deepest Well: Healing the Long-Term Effects of Childhood Adversity* (New York: Houghton Mifflin Harcourt, 2018), 21.

19. Edward A. Charlesworth and Ronald G. Nathan, *Stress Management: A Comprehensive Guide to Wellness* (New York: Ballantine Books, 2004), x.

20. "Coping with Stress," Centers for Disease Control and Prevention, last reviewed July 22, 2021, https://www.cdc.gov/mentalhealth/stress-cop ing/cope-with-stress/index.html.

21. "2017 Children's Mental Health Report," Child Mind Institute, 2017, https://childmind.org/report/2017-childrens-mental-health-report/.

22. Center for Adolescent Health, "Teen Stress," Johns Hopkins Bloomberg School of Public Health, 2009, https://www.jhsph.edu/research/cen ters-and-institutes/center-for-adolescent-health/_docs/policy-briefs /mental-health/teen_stress.pdf.

23. Russell D. Romeo, "The Teenage Brain: The Stress Response and the Adolescent Brain," *Current Directions in Psychological Science* 22, no. 2 (2013): 140–45, https://doi.org/10.1177/0963721413475445.

24. Romeo, "The Teenage Brain."

25. Harris, *The Deepest Well*, 38.

Chapter 3. Exploring Anxiety

1. "Terms A–Z," Child Mind Institute, https://childmind.org/glossary /#anxiety-disorders (accessed July 29, 2021).

2. "2018 Children's Mental Health Report," Child Mind Institute, 2018, https://childmind.org/awareness-campaigns/childrens-mental-health -report/2018-childrens-mental-health-report/.

3. World Health Organization, *The ICD-11 Classification of Mental and Behavioural Disorders: Clinical Descriptions and Diagnostic Guidelines*, Vol. 6 (Geneva: WHO, 2021), 42.

4. World Health Organization, *The ICD-11 Classification of Mental and Behavioural Disorders: Clinical Descriptions and Diagnostic Guidelines*, Vol. 21 (Geneva: WHO, 2021), 15.

5. Arthur J. Lurigio, "Panic Attacks," *Salem Press Encyclopedia of Health* (Pasadena, CA: Salem Press, 2019), http://search.ebscohost.com/login .aspx?direct=true&db=ers&AN=93872133&site=eds-live&scope=site.

6. Rachel Willimott, *Acceptance & Commitment Therapy for Anxiety Relief* (Emeryville, CA: Rockville Press, 2020), 6.

7. Willimott, *Acceptance & Commitment Therapy for Anxiety Relief*, 45.

Chapter 5. On Anger and Coping with the Fight Response

1. Susan David, *Emotional Agility: Get Unstuck, Embrace Change, and Thrive in Work and Life* (New York: Penguin Random House, 2016), 94.

2. Brené Brown, *Daring Greatly: How the Courage to Be Vulnerable Transforms the Way We Live, Love, Parent, and Lead* (New York: Penguin Random House, 2012), 33–34.

3. David, *Emotional Agility*, 85.

Chapter 6. On Discomfort and Coping with the Flight Response

1. Shelley E. Taylor, "Tend and Befriend Theory," in Paul A. M. Van Lange, Arie W. Kruglanski, and E. Tory Higgins (eds.), *The Handbook of Theories of Social Psychology* (London: Sage Publications, 2012), 33.

2. Susan David, *Emotional Agility: Get Unstuck, Embrace Change, and Thrive in Work and Life* (New York: Penguin Random House, 2016), 45.

3. David, *Emotional Agility*, 47.

Chapter 7. Effective Coping
through Community

1. Brené Brown, *Daring Greatly: How the Courage to Be Vulnerable Transforms the Way We Live, Love, Parent, and Lead* (New York: Penguin Random House, 2012), 8.
2. Kelly Pavelich and Barb Solish, "Introducing NAMI's Youth Task Force," *NAMI Voice*, 64 (Summer 2021).
3. World Health Organization, *The ICD-11 Classification of Mental and Behavioural Disorders: Clinical Descriptions and Diagnostic Guidelines*, Vol. 6 (Geneva: WHO, 2021), 43.
4. Kira M. Newman, "How Journaling Can Help You in Hard Times," Greater Good Science Center at the University of California Berkeley, August 18, 2020, https://greatergood.berkeley.edu/article/item/how_journaling_can_help_you_in_hard_times.
5. Elaine Aron, *The Highly Sensitive Person: How to Thrive When the World Overwhelms You* (New York: Harmony Books, 2016).
6. Aron, *The Highly Sensitive Person*, xvii.
7. Aron, *The Highly Sensitive Person*, 11.
8. Aron, *The Highly Sensitive Person*, xiii.
9. Aron, *The Highly Sensitive Person*, 18.
10. Susan Cain, *Quiet: The Power of Introverts in a World That Can't Stop Talking* (New York: Broadway Books, 2013), 4.
11. Margaret Mead, "Sex and Temperament in Three Primitive Societies," in Michael S. Kimmel and Amy Aronson (eds.), *The Gendered Society Reader* (London: Oxford University Press, 2000), 40–41.
12. Aron, *The Highly Sensitive Person*, 15.
13. Joseph L. Flanders, Vanessa Leo, Daniel Paquette, Robert O. Pihl, and Jean R. Séguin, "Rough-and-Tumble Play and the Regulation of Aggression: An Observational Study of Father-Child Play Dyads," *Aggressive Behavior* 35, no. 4 (2009): 285–95, https://doi.org/10.1002/ab.20309.
14. Cain, *Quiet*, 3.
15. Cain, *Quiet*, 3–4.
16. Cain, *Quiet*, 10.

CHAPTER 8. EFFECTIVE COPING THROUGH GRATITUDE

1. Emily Nagoski and Amelia Nagoski, *Burnout: The Secret to Unlocking the Stress Cycle* (New York: Penguin Random House, 2019), 209.
2. Brené Brown, *Daring Greatly: How the Courage to Be Vulnerable Transforms the Way We Live, Love, Parent, and Lead* (New York: Penguin Random House, 2012), 34.
3. Michael E. McCullough, Robert A. Emmons, and Jo-Ann Tsang, "The Grateful Disposition: A Conceptual and Empirical Topography," *Journal of Personality and Social Psychology*, 82, no. 1 (2012): 112–27, https://doi.org/10.1037/0022-3514.82.1.112.
4. Summer Allen, "The Science of Gratitude," The Greater Good Science Center at the University of California Berkeley, May 2018, https://ggsc.berkeley.edu/images/uploads/GGSC-JTF_White_Paper-Gratitude-FINAL.pdf, 8.
5. Allen, "The Science of Gratitude," 28.
6. Brown, *Daring Greatly*, 125.
7. Michael Y. Park, "A History of the Cake Mix, the Invention That Redefined 'Baking,'" *Bon Appetit*, September 26, 2013, https://www.bonappetit.com/entertaining-style/pop-culture/article/cake-mix-history.
8. Nagoski and Nagoski, *Burnout*, 209.

CHAPTER 9. PANDEMIC EXPERIENCES

1. "A Return to 'Normal': Assessing Mental Health Concerns Among U.S. Teens," Morgan Stanley Alliance for Children's Mental Health, August 2021, https://www.morganstanley.com/assets/pdfs/reemergence-program-teen-survey-factsheet.pdf, 5.

CHAPTER 11. COPING STRATEGIES: THOUGHTS

1. Kimberly Holland, "Amygdala Hijack: When Emotion Takes Over," *Healthline*, September 17, 2021, https://www.healthline.com/health/stress/amygdala-hijack.

BIBLIOGRAPHY

"2017 Children's Mental Health Report." Child Mind Institute, 2017. https://childmind.org/report/2017-childrens-mental-health-report/.

"2018 Children's Mental Health Report." Child Mind Institute, 2018. https://childmind.org/awareness-campaigns/childrens-mental -health-report/2018-childrens-mental-health-report/.

Allen, Summer. "The Science of Gratitude." The Greater Good Science Center at the University of California Berkeley, May 2018. https://ggsc.berkeley.edu/images/uploads/GGSC-JTF_White _Paper-Gratitude-FINAL.pdf.

Aron, Elaine. *The Highly Sensitive Person: How to Thrive When the World Overwhelms You*. New York: Harmony Books, 2016.

Associated Press. "Study: 'Time' Is Most Often Used Noun." *CBS News*, June 22, 2006. https://www.cbsnews.com/news/study-time-is -most-often-used-noun/.

Brosnan-Watters, Gayle L. "Fight-or-Flight Response." *Salem Press Encyclopedia of Health*. Pasadena, CA: Salem Press, 2019. http:// search.ebscohost.com/login.aspx?direct=true&db=ers&AN= 93871966&site=eds-live&scope=site.

Brown, Brené. *Daring Greatly: How the Courage to Be Vulnerable Transforms the Way We Live, Love, Parent, and Lead*. New York: Penguin Random House, 2012.

Cain, Susan. *Quiet: The Power of Introverts in a World That Can't Stop Talking*. New York: Broadway Books, 2013.

Center for Adolescent Health. "Teen Stress." Johns Hopkins Bloomberg School of Public Health, 2009. https://www.jhsph.edu/research

/centers-and-institutes/center-for-adolescent-health/_docs/policy
-briefs/mental-health/teen_stress.pdf.

Charlesworth, Edward A., and Ronald G. Nathan. *Stress Management:
A Comprehensive Guide to Wellness*. New York: Ballantine Books,
2004.

"Coping with Stress." Centers for Disease Control and Prevention,
last reviewed July 22, 2021. https://www.cdc.gov/mentalhealth
/stress-coping/cope-with-stress/index.html.

"CovEx Results." Centers for Disease Control and Prevention, last
reviewed March 18, 2021. https://www.cdc.gov/healthyyouth
/data/covex/Covex_results.htm.

David, Susan. *Emotional Agility: Get Unstuck, Embrace Change, and
Thrive in Work and Life*. New York: Penguin Random House, 2016.

DeSilver, Drew. "The Concerns and Challenges of Being a U.S. Teen:
What the Data Show." Pew Research Center, February 26, 2019.
https://www.pewresearch.org/fact-tank/2019/02/26/the-concerns
-and-challenges-of-being-a-u-s-teen-what-the-data-show/.

Flanders, Joseph L., Vanessa Leo, Daniel Paquette, Robert O. Pihl,
and Jean R. Séguin. "Rough-and-Tumble Play and the Regulation of Aggression: An Observational Study of Father-Child Play
Dyads." *Aggressive Behavior* 35, no. 4 (2009): 285–95. https://doi
.org/10.1002/ab.20309.

Goetsch, Virginia L., and Kevin T. Larkin. "Physiological Responses
to Stress." *Salem Press Encyclopedia of Health*. Pasadena, CA:
Salem Press, 2019. http://search.ebscohost.com/login.aspx?direct
=true&db=ers&AN=93872155&site=eds-live&scope=site.

Harris, Nadine Burke. *The Deepest Well: Healing the Long-Term Effects of
Childhood Adversity*. New York: Houghton Mifflin Harcourt, 2018.

Holland, Kimberly. "Amygdala Hijack: When Emotion Takes Over."
Healthline, September 17, 2021. https://www.healthline.com
/health/stress/amygdala-hijack.

Immordino-Yang, Mary Helen, Joanna A. Christodoulou, and Vanessa
Singh. "Rest Is Not Idleness: Implications of the Brain's Default
Mode for Human Development and Education." *Perspectives on*

Psychological Science 7, no. 4 (July 2012): 352–64. https://doi .org/10.1177/1745691612447308.

Jaret, Peter. "The Surprising Benefits of Stress." The Greater Good Science Center at the University of California Berkeley, October 20, 2015. https://greatergood.berkeley.edu/article/item/the_sur prising_benefits_of_stress.

Krapić, Nada, Jasna Hudek-Knezevic, and Igor Kardum. "Stress in Adolescence: Effects on Development." *International Encyclopedia of the Social & Behavioral Sciences*. Amsterdam: Elsevier, 2015. https:// doi.org/10.1016/B978-0-08-097086-8.23031-6.

Lurigio, Arthur J. "Panic Attacks." *Salem Press Encyclopedia of Health*. Pasadena, CA: Salem Press, 2019. http://search.ebscohost.com /login.aspx?direct=true&db=ers&AN=93872133&site=eds-live &scope=site.

McCullough, Michael E., Robert A. Emmons, and Jo-Ann Tsang. "The Grateful Disposition: A Conceptual and Empirical Topography." *Journal of Personality and Social Psychology* 82, no. 1 (2012): 112–27. https://doi.org/10.1037/0022-3514.82.1.112.

Mead, Margaret. "Sex and Temperament in Three Primitive Societies." In *The Gendered Society Reader*, edited by Michael S. Kimmel and Amy Aronson, 40–41. London: Oxford University Press, 2000.

Nagoski, Emily, and Amelia Nagoski. *Burnout: The Secret to Unlocking the Stress Cycle*. New York: Penguin Random House, 2019.

Newman, Kira M. "How Journaling Can Help You in Hard Times." The Greater Good Science Center at the University of California Berkeley, August 18, 2020. https://greatergood.berkeley.edu /article/item/how_journaling_can_help_you_in_hard_times.

Osgood, Kelsey, Hannah Sheldon-Dean, and Henry Kimball. "2021 Children's Mental Health Report." Child Mind Institute, 2021. https://childmind.org/awareness-campaigns/childrens-mental -health-report/2021-childrens-mental-health-report/.

Park, Michael Y. "A History of the Cake Mix, the Invention That Redefined 'Baking.'" *Bon Appetit*, September 26, 2013. https://www

.bonappetit.com/entertaining-style/pop-culture/article/cake-mix
-history.

Pavelich, Kelly, and Barb Solish. "Introducing NAMI's Youth Task
Force." *NAMI Voice*, 64 (Summer 2021).

Piotrowski, Nancy A., and David Wason Hollar, Jr. "Stress." *Magill's
Medical Guide Online Edition*. Pasadena, CA: Salem Press, 2019.
http://search.ebscohost.com/login.aspx?direct=true&db=ers
&AN=89093561&site=eds-live&scope=site.

"Prevalence of Any Anxiety Disorder among Adolescents." National
Institute of Mental Health. https://www.nimh.nih.gov/health
/statistics/any-anxiety-disorder#part_2578 (accessed October 4,
2021).

Rajan, Amol. "OED Word of the Year expanded for 'unprecedented'
2020." *BBC News*, November 23, 2020. https://www.bbc.com
/news/entertainment-arts-55016543.

"A Return to 'Normal': Assessing Mental Health Concerns Among U.S.
Teens." Morgan Stanley Alliance for Children's Mental Health,
August 2021. https://www.morganstanley.com/assets/pdfs/reemer
gence-program-teen-survey-factsheet.pdf.

Romeo, Russell D. "The Teenage Brain: The Stress Response and the
Adolescent Brain." *Current Directions in Psychological Science* 22, no.
2 (2013): 140–45. https://doi.org/10.1177/0963721413475445.

Schaeffer, Katherine. "Most U.S. Teens Who Use Cellphones Do It
to Pass Time, Connect With Others, Learn New Things." Pew
Research Center, August 23, 2019. https://www.pewresearch.org
/fact-tank/2019/08/23/most-u-s-teens-who-use-cellphones-do-it
-to-pass-time-connect-with-others-learn-new-things/.

Taylor, Shelley E. "Tend and Befriend Theory." In *The Handbook of
Theories of Social Psychology*, edited by Paul A. M. Van Lange, Arie
W. Kruglanski, and E. Tory Higgins, 32–47. London: Sage Publi-
cations, 2012.

"Terms A–Z." Child Mind Institute. https://childmind.org/glossary
/#anxiety-disorders (accessed July 29, 2021).

Willimott, Rachel. *Acceptance & Commitment Therapy for Anxiety Relief.* Emeryville, CA: Rockville Press, 2020.

World Health Organization. *The ICD-11 Classification of Mental and Behavioural Disorders: Clinical Descriptions and Diagnostic Guidelines,* Vol. 6. Geneva: WHO, 2021.

———. *The ICD-11 Classification of Mental and Behavioural Disorders: Clinical Descriptions and Diagnostic Guidelines,* Vol. 21. Geneva: WHO, 2021.

Zimmer, Scott. "Oxytocin." *Salem Press Encyclopedia of Health.* Pasadena, CA: Salem Press, 2020. http://search.ebscohost.com/login.aspx?direct=true&db=ers&AN=87324180&site=eds-live&scope=site.

INDEX

211.org, 56. *See also* resources for help

abuse, 11, 26, 28–29, 40, 66, 76, 91;
anecdotes addressing, 83–85; and
crisis resources, 54–56, 141–42. *See
also* resources for help
academics: anecdotes addressing stress
with, 15–19, 36, 25–26, 32–34,
36, 47–49, 80, 83–84, 109–14; and
pandemic impact on, xi–xiv, 25–26,
32–34; and schools as safe space,
26–27; as stressor, 6, 23, 28–29, 47,
125, 128, 130
ADHD, 26; anecdotes addressing, 83–84
alcohol abuse, 31, 76, 137; anecdotes
addressing, 79–81, 83–84. *See also*
drug abuse; flight response; substance
abuse
American Psychiatric Association, 44
anger, 29, 31, 65–70, 91, 101, 133;
anecdotes addressing, 70–74,
85, 112–13; and effective
communication, 70; and feelings
versus behavior, 66–67; as secondary
emotion, 67–68, 103
anxiety, xiv, xv, 25–26, 31, 39, 43–52,
53–54, 65, 90–92, 95–96, 99,
109; necdotes addressing, 14–18,
47–51; diagnostic criteria for, 43–45;
as healthy, 43; physical signs of,
135–36; and thought patterns, 62,
124–25. *See also* panic attacks; social
anxiety
Aron, Elaine N., 96

autism: anecdotes addressing, 14–17, 95;
and pandemic impact on, 26

BIPOC: and pandemic impact on, 26;
resources for support, 143–44. *See
also* racism
body image, 24; anecdotes addressing,
34–36
brain function and habits, 65, 92,
97, 102, 105, 137; and adolescent
development of, 39–40; and the
amygdala hijack, 123–25; and brain
break benefits, x; effect of stress on,
3, 8, 31, 39; and role in controlling
stress response, 5–6, 8–10, 12; and
thinking errors, 125–31
Brown, Brené, 24–25, 67–68, 89, 103
bullying, 29, 91; anecdotes addressing,
34–35, 37, 83–84

Cain, Susan, 97–98
cancer: anecdotes addressing, 38, 59–60
chronic stress, 27–32, 40, 53, 57, 65,
92; anecdotes addressing, 34–38;
definition of, 27; medical issues
caused by, 30–31; symptoms of, 31.
See also stress
coping skills: anecdotes addressing,
21, 41, 57–60; and strategies
for physical health, 135–37; and
community, 89–99; and strategies for
emotional health, 133–34; and fight
response, 65–74; and flight response,
75–87; and gratitude, 101–6; and

National Alliance on Mental Illness
(nami.org), 55, 56, 140, 142. *See also*
resources for help
natural disasters, xv–xvi, 24–25;
anecdotes addressing, 115–19
non-binary identity: anecdotes
addressing, 37. *See also* LGBTQ+

OK2Talk (ok2talk.org),143. *See also*
resources for help
oxytocin, 9–10

pandemic. *See* COVID-19
panic attacks, 8, 25, 44–47, 65;
anecdotes addressing, 15, 50–51;
definition of, 45; symptoms of, 47.
See also anxiety

racism, 17; anecdotes addressing, 18; and
BIPOC support, 143–44
relationships. *See* dating; family
dynamics; friendship dynamics
remote learning and socializing, xiii–xiv,
23, 62; anecdotes addressing, 17,
32–34, 38, 58, 113–14
resources for help, 54–57, 139–44

school. *See* academics
self-harm, 66; and crisis resources, 54–56,
139–44. *See also* resources for help
sex, 76; and pressure or abuse, 40
sexuality. *See* LGBTQ+
social anxiety, xv, 25, 44, 95–96, 109;
anecdotes addressing, 14–17;
definition of, 90; and pandemic
impact on, 26, 89–90
social isolation, 26, 62, 68, 89–91, 97;
and negative impact on health, 9, 89.
See also support systems; tend-and-
befriend response
social media, 24, 68, 77, 130; and
anecdotes addressing, 36–37,
112–13, 117

stress: as beneficial, 3–4, 10–11, 27;
definition of, 3; and long-term
effects, 4–5, 27–32; as more intense
during adolescence, 4, 6, 38–40; and
physiological effects, 3, 8–9, 29–31;
as result of change, 3–4, 6, 23, 27,
38, 47; as survival adaptation, 3,
27–28; as variable, 11–12, 14. *See also*
chronic stress; fight-or-flight response;
stressors; tend-and-befriend response
stressors, 4, 5–6, 8–9, 11–14, 23, 32,
38–40, 41, 65, 75, 89; anecdotes
addressing, 34–38; and anxiety,
43–45; common types of, 6;
definition of, 3; and early humans,
27–30; and identification of, 65–68,
124, 135–36; and modern challenges,
23–25, 28–30; and panic attacks, 47.
See also anxiety; panic attacks; stress
substance abuse, 76, 79–84. *See also*
alcohol abuse; drug abuse; flight
response
suicide: and crisis resources, 54–56,
139–44. *See also* resources for help
support systems, 25–26, 66, 89–92;
anecdotes addressing, 57–60, 93–95;
and positive impact on health, 9;
and reaching out, 53–57. *See also*
oxytocin; tend-and-befriend response

technology: and impact on stress, 23–24
tend-and-befriend response, 9, 12, 26–27,
29, 89–92, 95–96; definition of, 9
therapists. *See* mental health professionals
therapy. *See* mental health professionals
The Trevor Project, 143. *See also*
resources for help; LGBTQ+

weight. *See* body image
World Health Organization, 44

Zoom. *See* remote learning and
socializing

ABOUT THE AUTHOR

Christie Cognevich is an educator and writer based in New Orleans, Louisiana. She holds a PhD in English literature and taught literature, composition, and creative writing at the high school and university level for over a decade. She is the author of *Depression: Insights and Tips for Teenagers*.